"A fun ride from Apprentice to Business Grandmaster. Grab it!"
—Donald Trump

"Three moves ahead? I'd say four, at least. An utterly fresh guide to winning in today's business environment."
—Jim Spanfeller, CEO, Forbes.com

"Every executive struggles with the pressure to think fast and think ahead. Bob's fascinating book shows how to apply chess principles to do just that. It's impossible to make the right move every time, but these strategies will help you succeed in the face of the unpredictable."
—Bruce Chizen, former CEO, Adobe Systems Incorporated

"This amazing book is the first time anyone has clearly translated Grandmaster ideas to real-world situations. The business examples are so good that I'm using them to teach chess!"
—Maurice Ashley, International Chess

"Rarely does one find a book where every page is filled with both brilliant insight and witty writing. Mandatory reading for every startup."
—David S. Rose, founder, New York Angels

"I don't play chess but it sure improved my 'game' at the office! The clever, clear examples show how to use dozens of classic strategies in everyday situations. This book can put any executive 'three moves ahead'!"
—Sarah Fay, CEO, Carat USA

THREE MOVES AHEAD

THREE MOVES AHEAD

What Chess Can Teach You About Business (Even If You've Never Played)

Bob Rice

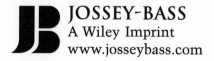

JOSSEY-BASS
A Wiley Imprint
www.josseybass.com

Published by Jossey-Bass
A Wiley Imprint
989 Market Street, San Francisco, CA 94103-1741—www.josseybass.com

Jossey-Bass books and products are available through most bookstores. To contact Jossey-Bass directly
call our Customer Care Department within the U.S. at 800-956-7739, outside the U.S. at 317-572-3986,
or fax 317-572-4002.

Jossey-Bass also publishes its books in a variety of electronic formats. Some content that appears in
print may not be available in electronic books.

Library of Congress Cataloging-in-Publication Data

Rice, Robert, 1954-
    Three moves ahead : what chess can teach you about business (even if you've never played) /
  Robert Rice.
      p. cm.
    Includes bibliographical references and index.
    ISBN 978-0-470-17821-8 (cloth)
    1. Strategic planning. 2. Success in business. 3. Decision making. 4. Chess—Psychological aspects.
  I. Title.
  HD30.28.R498 2008
  658.4'012—dc22   2007050894

Printed in the United States of America
FIRST EDITION
HB Printing   10 9 8 7 6 5 4 3 2 1

CONTENTS

To Lenore, my best move, and our two great wins, Eric and Isabelle

PREFACE

As it turns out, information age business comes with a 1,000-year-old user's guide.

That's fortunate, for our suddenly flat world is inflicting business disruptions of historic proportions. It has obliterated many of the traditional barriers to entry: physical plant, local suppliers, and guarded relationships. It has amped up the volume of information to deafening levels. It has introduced new competitors from places we didn't even know existed. It has compressed the time for making decisions and shortened every sort of business cycle, from product launches to stock turnover time to CEO life spans. Intellectual property, not physical property, has become the weapon of choice.

This wave has overwhelmed standard business analytical tools. Nearly all of these involve some variation of reducing possible choices to their present economic values, with the one that generates the biggest number winning. Problem is, doing that requires the business equivalent of a giant sloth: the kind of slow-moving, predictable market that is now nearly extinct. To a radically greater degree than ever before, today's strategic and operational decisions must be made without a clear understanding of their outcomes. That is, to compete successfully in the "information revolution," *you have to know what to do when you're not sure what to do.* Chess teaches that. And that's why the greatest strategy and knowledge game in human history is so relevant to today's business issues.

In the following pages, you'll see how great companies in every industry, from Adobe to 3M, and from start-ups to conglomerates, use these strategies to compete effectively in our wildly unpredictable world. Many of them are proven offensive and defensive principles for attacking and defending markets, some demonstrate how to get new ventures off the ground, while others illustrate how to maximize and revitalize a withering advantage. Several relate to building efficient organizations, a handful show how to maintain momentum while under attack, and still others help you choose among reasonable alternatives while under pressure.

All have proved effective over centuries of competition by brilliant minds, so you can be pretty confident that they're correct. Should you doubt that, just look at how profoundly the game has always reflected and informed the major aspects of society.

The "DaVinci Code" of the late middle ages, the blowout blockbuster of the pre-movable type days, was *Book of the Customs of Men and the Duties of Nobles.* The killer title alone didn't account for its success.[1] Written by an Italian monk, it tells the story of a king so wicked that he hacked his father into 300 pieces and fed him to the vultures. Fortunately, in the big plot twist, he then learned the game of chess. That redeemed him, for the formerly evil one came to understand that his position was utterly dependent on the society functioning as a whole and the performance of its lowliest members.

The author portrayed the individual pawns as blacksmiths, innkeepers, messengers, and the like, and the more important Knights, Bishops, Castles, and Queens played themselves. This medieval morality play proved so popular over such a long period that it was translated from Latin into French, Italian, Dutch, Spanish, Swedish, English, and German and even earned 20 editions after the printing press was invented 150 years later.

Indeed, the game has always served as a mirror of intellectual and societal evolution and often as a precursor of important developments. Before *Customs of Men,* for example, it had been a religious lesson. The pieces came out of the same bag, sprang to life for a while during the game, and then all went back into the same bag together. Regardless of your worldly situation, a return to God, from whence you came, leveled the experience.

Later, chess prophesized political developments. Perhaps its most prescient moment came in the late 1700s, when the great French player Philador observed that "Pawns are the soul of chess."

That was as revolutionary a thought for chess theory, sparking a profound reevaluation of proper play, as it was about to be in French politics. If Marie Antoinette had just checked out the Café Regence, trendy hotspot of the chess world, she might well have been a little less cavalier in her unfortunate suggestions about dietary substitutions.

Even social moods and customs have been played out on the board. The swashbuckling, territory-conquering 1800s gave rise to the "romantic period" in chess, during which no self-respecting, man's man would fail to offer a risky gambit or to accept one. Next came the Classical period, which rejected these "unsound" romantic ideas in favor of a model featuring rigorous rules about the "proper" way to play, which very much echoed the staid mores of Victorian England.

Then came a surprising pas de deux between science and chess. At the end of the nineteenth century, scientists were concluding that Newtonian physics had essentially answered all the big questions and that the discipline had no future. At the same time, Grandmasters lamented that all the secrets of the chessboard had been found: World champion Emanuel Lasker complained that the game had been studied so much that all the correct moves were understood.

And then earthquakes hit both disciplines. Albert Einstein's "miracle year" of 1905 upended Newtonian classicism with his theory of relativity and the idea of the "quantum" (later spawning the uncertainty principle, a concept relevant to this book). The chess echo came from the "Hypermodernists" of the 1920s. Steinitz, the chess world's Newton, had long before set down the "universal law" that early occupation of the center of the board was the key to winning chess games. But the Hypermodernists dared their opponents to do just that while they sat back and attacked from the wings and corners. This shocking challenge to orthodoxy proved just as influential to chess theory as relativity would to physics.

At the same time, similar revolutions arose against classicism in art, theater, and government. One of those, the Russian Revolution, intensified the interplay between human events and the (formerly) "royal game" when the Soviets seized the game as a symbol of communist superiority.

The Soviet School successfully produced a tide of dreary, oppressive technocrats who dominated world play for decades. The style was built on the excruciatingly slow buildup of pressure, incrementally overpowering opponents while taking no risks. Then, once again playing political pundit, the game signaled the beginning of the end of the Cold War when Bobby Fischer unseated Boris Spassky as champ in 1972, an event second only to the "Miracle on Ice" for sporting ignominy in Russia. Although the old Soviets were able to regain control of the game briefly when Fischer abdicated his throne (believing, among other things, that Martians were sending radio signals to the filings in his teeth), the coup de grace was ultimately delivered from within by Garry Kasparov, an Azerbaijani Jew who was the antithesis of the regime personally, politically, and stylistically.

Even though Kasparov was indisputably the greatest player in history, his outsider status generated overwhelming state resistance. The KGB spied on his match preparations to better equip his opponents, and the Russian government conspired with the world chess authorities to cancel a world championship match just as he was about to pull off the greatest comeback in sports history. He overcame these obstacles to become the ultimate anti-Soviet champion and fittingly reigned over the chess world as the old order collapsed. His current political activism is just a continuation of his brave career.

Chess has thus always mirrored, and even predicted, civilization's dominant themes. Especially given the fundamental role that business has assumed in the world's social order, it would be shocking, indeed, if the game failed to provide important lessons for modern executives.

So, let's see what this "user's guide" has to say.

THREE MOVES AHEAD

CHAPTER ONE

THE WALL STREET CHESS CLUB

A couple of years before quite accidentally becoming its CEO, I ran business development for a small public company. It was the 1990s, we had some cool graphics software, and I was headed to Redmond to sell it to Microsoft . . . or so I thought.

After years of work and interminable reviews by their technical experts, we believed our moment of glory had finally arrived. We expected that soon we'd announce a huge transaction with the industry leader, rake in a fortune, and watch our stock rocket.

But then the meeting actually started. My Microsoft counterpart opened the proceedings by reading me what he called, with absolutely no sign of a smile, the "rules of engagement" for dealing with his company. Turns out, these were essentially a corporate version of the Miranda rights, the ones police have to read when they arrest you. (Actually, that was only fair: Bill Gates is a lot scarier to a small technology company than the local sheriff.)

Instead of the right to remain silent, you had the right to not do business with them at all; it was, mercifully, still possible to just leave. If, however, you did decide to proceed, two things were absolute: one, Microsoft would own your software lock, stock, and barrel; and two, you would be paid absolutely nothing for it.

Hmm. Well, this was not exactly the sort of shrewd deal that I expected to win me a bonus. In fact, it didn't: I almost got fired for accepting.

Whatever possessed me to say yes? My chess gut said it was time for an "exchange sacrifice." Now, for some reason, that particular explanation didn't completely mollify the unruly crowd back at the office. Even the famously practiced L.A. cool of our black-tee-and-shades CEO got blown, reportedly causing him to bang up his IPO Porsche when he got the news via cell phone. So, forced to defend this "little brilliancy" to the entire board of directors, I tried a different approach.

Look, hard as it was to swallow, what Microsoft was saying was true: that we could only become a major company if our software reached enough people to make a difference, and that could only happen through them. Well, correct, we could not continue licensing our desktop software to companies once it was free as part of Windows, so, yes, we would have to find an entirely new business model . . . and, no, we hadn't quite worked that one out yet. To the board, unfortunately, I was unable to repeat the Microsoft guy's detailed analysis on this point: if, with this new Internet thing happening, we weren't smart enough to find a way to monetize the fact that our software would be on tens of millions of machines, he reasoned, "You suck."

So it boiled down to two options. We could continue to license our code for a few dollars here and there and risk slowly becoming passé, or we could get it into use by many millions of users quickly (albeit for free) and find some new way to play in the next, Internet phase of the game. Even though we couldn't exactly see how to exploit the distribution, and even though it meant junking the model that had paid the rent, we had to go for it—what chess players would call an exchange sacrifice—trading one kind of advantage for a completely different sort, even though the exact benefits can't be calculated.

And, fortunately, the plan more or less worked. We did get our software onto more than half of all computers in the U.S., and we did figure out a new business model based on that fact, although in the short run, it didn't generate enough revenue to replace what we gave up. Instead, as is the idea with this kind of move, the real payoff came later: The new model propelled us directly into what would become the white-hot Internet advertising business, in a way that the old one never could have. Meantime, nearly all the graphics companies that stuck to their old desktop business models died on the vine as the Web blossomed.

Brilliant long-term planning? Hardly. But it wasn't pure luck, either. We did figure that this "Internet thing" just might be a hit, but we had no more idea than anyone else how Web advertising would evolve. Nonetheless, we wound up ideally positioned for it. We didn't have a crystal ball, but we were playing chess.

It's often that way: the best business moves come right off the board. Indeed, what's amazing is how many chess principles are directly applicable to the world of business and how they can help executives make the right move in so many situations—with strategic development, of course, but also when attacking competitors, defending turf, cracking new markets, and, well, in just about every aspect of running a business these days.

The idea for this book began to dawn on me long before my stint as the biz dev guy (and later, CEO) of that software company, back when I was still a lawyer, while scanning the audience at a world championship match between Garry Kasparov and Anatoly Karpov in New York's Macklowe Hotel in 1992. The room was absolutely teeming with famous Wall Street guys, some I knew from my practice down there, some were stars I'd never met: George Soros, Steve Friedman (head of Goldman, Sachs), and Jimmy Cayne, who ran Bear, Stearns. Was that an accident or a clue?

That question sparked the creation of the Wall Street Chess Club. And what a club it became. On our very first night, we got the above luminaries as well as a virtual "who's who" from all the other Wall Street shops. Word spread through the chess circles of New York's large Russian émigré community, which had recently been supplemented by a huge influx of top Grandmasters (GMs) who bailed out as things got shaky in the old Soviet Union. Soon we were nearly overrun by top players. I guess their usual clubs didn't offer fine red wines and gourmet sandwiches or feature expansive views over the Statue of Liberty in the harbor far below. But for whatever reason, we suddenly had the strongest club in the world.

Among the regulars and guests were ex-world champions Tal, Spassky, and Karpov; other "super GMs" like Dzindzichashvili (later my teacher), Albert, and Kamsky; the American stars Ashley, Rhode, Benjamen, Seriwan, and Wolff; the rage of the chess world, the three Hungarian Polgar sisters; and eventually, the greatest player ever and reigning world champion, Kasparov himself.

The running joke was that the executives were coming to learn to play chess, and the chess players were coming to learn to make money. But the communities blended very well indeed, and many players ultimately took jobs at the investment houses, often as traders; Banker's Trust actually launched a formal recruiting effort to bring in GMs.

So the question was answered. Chess and business did indeed share a deep connection.

Soon thereafter, Kasparov asked me to help him start the Professional Chess Association, a rival to the then-worldwide governing body of chess. We staged all sorts of events in unusual venues with unique formats, including the first commercial event ever held inside the Kremlin (during which our sponsor got more than its money's worth when a well-placed gratuity got the "Intel Inside" logo projected on the outside walls for a night, an image that was flashed all over the globe); a world championship played atop the World Trade Center; and a "speed chess" TV series hosted by Maurice Ashley for ESPN.

But the life-changing event occurred later, when Kasparov introduced me to a brilliant Russian physicist, Sasha Migdal, a Princeton professor who had invented a three-dimensional camera (I'll explain later). Blinded by the possibilities, I quit the practice of law and jumped into a true start-up. That's when I got my chance to put chess theory into business practice.

Fortunately, I didn't know a thing about the basic rules of business at the time. If I had, I'd still be a lawyer because one of those rules probably says to make sure you have a viable product before you leave a cushy job and bet the farm on it. Much to my dismay, it turned out that there was actually no demand at all for what we were selling—and just about the only good news about that was that it didn't turn out to matter much, as the product didn't actually work so terribly well, anyway.

But, because we "played chess," things turned out OK. We went into a "deep think" about our position after an embarrassing series of setbacks (including, in a heavily promoted stunt, posting 3D pictures of all the Miss Universe contestants on the NBC Web site the night of the show. Our expected tour de force turned into a disaster because the then-nonstandard systems for displaying 3D on the Web rendered these gorgeous women as mangled Picassos on everybody's computers except ours, and we were almost sued by Miss Argentina). We decided to play our first "exchange sac" by jettisoning the camera and relying on the underlying algorithms to develop graphics software for the Internet. We then pursued a "first-mover advantage," "castled early," established a "strong square" in Web 3D, and got bought by a public company.

Of which I became CEO at the exact moment that the fantastic Internet bubble burst, taking our stock price and most of our customers with it. Our game hung by a thread. But we went on, one move at a time, not knowing what the endgame would be. We just kept making the next best move we could find, accumulating small advantages and trading them for others, until suddenly the winning path, Internet advertising, emerged.

The more or less happy result ensued largely because I had one piece of training most MBAs don't: my sister Dianne had taught me to play chess as a kid, and the Bobby Fischer match made it stick.

But, as you've seen, that didn't equip me to predict the future. Despite what most nonplayers believe, winning at chess is *not* based on the skill of seeing ahead 15 moves (or, as we'll see, even three).

Nor, fortunately, is it about IQ, another common misconception. We might as well pop that bubble right now: most great chess players are of average intelligence. Sure, some people are naturally more talented at the game than others, just as some folks learn to play the piano or speak a foreign language faster than most, but none of these mental skills means beans about how "smart" you are in the typical sense of the word. Anyone can become competent at chess, just as they can at music or language, simply by learning and practicing the basic principles.

No, far from being a dry science of pure calculation and certain foresight, world class chess is about having a plan to generate an advantage but prosecuting it in a flexible way; at the right moment, swapping that advantage for one of a different sort, and then doing it again; moving quickly even when you're not exactly sure what to do; making intelligent sacrifices; taking risks; believing in yourself; and dealing with the present, not the past.

That said, there are, of course, several concrete strategies and tactics to understand; that's what the book is about. These methods do not banish uncertainty, but they do position you to take advantage of it. They set you up for "unexpected" success.

After all, these strategies and tactics guided an outsider, a country-bumpkin lawyer like me (who, when introduced to Leon Black not only asked what he did for a living but followed up with "And what's an investment banker?"), into position to become a partner at one of the most prestigious law firm on Wall Street, which led to the Wall Street Chess Club, which in turn led to my running that event in the Kremlin. This then gave me the chance to launch a start-up with the guy who solved two-dimensional quantum gravity theory (and whose father created the Russian hydrogen bomb), which then, despite the Miss Universe fiasco, got acquired by a screenwriter's exaggerated version of a wacky West Coast public company. My annointment as CEO of that company happened mostly because the board figured I'd play better in an accidentally scheduled "Power Lunch" interview than my seriously surfer dude predecessor.

So, you can see, my career path wasn't exactly a 15-moves-ahead type deal. Instead, it happened precisely because I didn't have a long-term fixed plan to disrupt. The basic principles of good play—get a big idea, use it to build an advantage, improve it, swap it out for a new one, move quickly, see what happens, make a new plan, and move again—worked on a professional level just as much as they do in corporate warfare.

Indeed, the more you look at the business world, the more you see that successful companies and the people who run them use chess strategies routinely (whether they know it or not): to create strategy, manage people, make decisions, and most of all, cope with the rapidly increasing rate of change in the world, with the unknowable future.

CHAPTER TWO

THREE MOVES AHEAD?

I bet you've heard a friend say, "I like chess, but I'm not very good at it because I can only see two or three moves ahead." Probably you didn't think much about it at the time, but what's your apparently modest buddy actually saying here?

Well, in an average chess position, there are about 40 possible moves, so seeing one full move ahead (yours and your opponent's response) would involve 1,600 positions (40 × 40). If we take that to the breathtaking number of two moves out, your friend is claiming that he's seeing over 2.5 million positions. Three moves? Four billion. The guy's totally full of himself! How do you put up with him?

Just one more minute on the math. Because an average game lasts 40 moves, one can fairly easily calculate the number of unique games to be on the order of 10^{128}. That is hugely larger than the number of known atoms in the universe, which, as Fred Friedel, the godfather of the world's chess community, points out, is a "pitiful" 10^{80}.

We won't dwell on the amazing fact that humans can still beat supercomputers at such a game, or how their techniques for doing so can help you manage a business amid the even more incalculable uncertainties of the information revolution. That's what most of this book is about, so we have time. However, what is essential, right up front, is to chew on the question of what it means to "see ahead," in chess and in business.

First, perhaps you think the number-waving above is overly dramatic; some of those possible moves, after all, would be inherently foolish. Sure, but ponder this: A substantial percentage of the smartest people of the past few hundred years have collectively played billions of games, and yet, there is still no consensus about the best way to even *start* the battle. I remember one game in the 1990 world championship in which Garry Kasparov absolutely shocked Anatoly Karpov, along with the 1,000 spectators in the hall, by opening a game with the Scotch, a system known since 1750 but that had not been played in a world championship match in more than a century. Karpov, himself among the handful of best players ever, was stunned by a line of play a quarter-millennium old. The point was not merely surprise: On a deep review of the opening, Kasparov had discovered some new ideas he wanted to try out. Even such an ancient system, picked over for hundreds of years by the best players, could produce brand new possibilities.

Indeed, the apparently precisely knowable world of chess is so unknowable in practice that ideas about the "right" way to play have ebbed and flowed over the years in parallel with other ongoing human battles with the unknown: art, politics, theater, and military science.

What does all this mean for us? One point is this: Despite the fundamentally limited options presented by an eight-by-eight squares board with just six different kinds of pieces and hundreds of years of thought by our smartest folks, there is not a single best way to play. Ideas and styles change. There are no sure-fire recipes for success.

But, chess *has* refined a set of principles over hundreds of years that show how to conduct an organizational battle in a hyperdynamic environment, where the future is unknowable (three moves is four billion positions) and the situation changes with every move—a challenge, one might say, very much like that faced by executives caught in the roiling uncertainties of today's information revolution.

After all, if we can't accurately forecast the course of a simple chess game, so narrow in comparison to real life, how can we do so for something as complex as a business in this environment? We can't. Or at least we can't in the way that people have usually thought about planning a business, with detailed long-term budgets and clear views about the future competitive landscape. That may have worked for Ma Bell in the fifties, but as its collapse demonstrated, such thinking simply cannot work in today's world. Instead, we need to grapple with the uncertainties, to "play business" like Grandmasters.

Fine, fine, fine, but does chess really have anything concrete to offer executives? Aside from bromides like "think ahead" and "move with a purpose," what does it bring to the party? To answer that, let's see who's already arrived at our little business advice get-together.

A trip down the business aisle at Borders will yield a book that preaches maniacal discipline . . . right next to one insisting on lightning agility. There's a manual of execution alongside a gospel of innovation. Here's one demanding a laser focus on core competencies, while its neighbor beseeches the development of breakthrough products. Some call for aggressive leadership; others dictate a quiet, collaborative style. Some demand breakneck speed, and some advise gradual change. Apparently each of these deeply contradictory formulas is the key to success.

On first reading, many of these tomes seem persuasive. But mostly they share a fundamentally flawed methodology. The usual formula is this: find several companies that have done well; identify a few characteristics they have in common; and conclude that if readers do these things, too, they'll find similar success. Although the best of this genre, such as Tom Peter's *In Search of Excellence* and Jim Collins's *Built to Last,* do offer worthy insights and ideas, they suffer from the same profound logical flaw. And it is this: *Thousands of companies that also shared the touted characteristics were complete failures.* Moreover, a review of the companies featured in such books a few years after publication speaks even louder about the "rules" they were following: would you really like your company to be like Digital Equipment, Wang, Polaroid, or K-Mart?

Aside from the basically flawed methodology, the problem with many such books is that they ignore the wildly variable contexts in which businesses find themselves. For many companies, trying to apply the lessons of such books would be like a new motorcycle owner reading instructions for riding a bicycle—vaguely similar, yes, but good luck when you try to brake by backpedaling. What behavior, for example, can be learned by studying the success of YouTube? Certainly, one would conclude by the financial success of the founders that it must have done a lot of things right. But if you followed those steps exactly today, with the same kind of management philosophy, you'd get creamed; the circumstances leading to its success were simply too unusual. The truth is that an idea that's worked once, or even several times, may well have zero precedential value for subsequent businesses.

Finally, readers of recipe-for-success books often fail to produce a nice cake for a simple reason. In the kitchen, there are rarely opponents who fight you tooth and nail for access to the springform pan. Most business advice books do not account for this fact. Instead, they preach that internal factors are primarily responsible for an entity's success. But in real life, someone's over there playing the Black pieces, and she gets just as many moves as you do.

Of course, a company's internal health is certainly a factor. But lots of companies with great quality control, focus, and customer-centric cultures fail because of events outside their control: the market, competitors, new technologies, changed government regulations, and a long list of other reasons. Regardless of how many companies with good internal dynamics do become successful, such factors are only one ingredient of success. How you play the ever-changing external world is certainly as important.

And the stocking of those bookstore aisles is finally beginning to reflect this. The best-seller list is shifting from tomes of sure-footed advice, guaranteed to work in every situation, to ruminations on the rate of change, the level of unpredictability, and the impact of happenstance: *The World Is Flat, The Tipping Point, The Innovator's Dilemma, The Black Swan,* and *The Halo Effect.*[1–5]

* * *

So the trip to the bookstore didn't work out. Maybe we should have gone to business school instead? Alas, a quick tour of the history of corporate strategy as taught in the leading business schools is a little like being back in Borders.

It's probably fair to say that the three essential aspects of any business are, one, what market it is fighting for; two, how the entity is organized and equipped to conduct the battle for that market; and three, how it deals with competitors, change, and the intrusion of the unexpected. And these, in turn, were the dominant topics of MBA training over the past 30 years. The first point, "What industry should you be in?" was the central theme of the early eighties. Because certain markets are inherently more profitable than others, the thinking went, please direct your attention there.

The second push revolved around "competing on capabilities." At this point, the focus moved from an industry-level focus to a company-centric one; it became fashionable to identify "core competencies" and to become a "learning organization." The shift became so pronounced that one could assume success would follow naturally from any well-run company, regardless of the industry it was in or who its competitors were. As noted above, this aspect of corporate strategic thinking is still heavily represented in the popular press.

Predictably, the pendulum then swung back. In the third wave, the catchphrase became "competing on resources," which essentially combined the first two big ideas: Success really depended on applying capabilities to the markets and competitors (the "environmental factors") it was trying to attack.

Meantime, from outside the lines came some basic questions about how corporate strategy should—or even could—be developed. "Logical incrementalism" challenged the basic idea that companies could systematically develop and implement strategies at all (and despite its proponents' protestations that they were not prescribing willful muddling, they were prescribing willful muddling). A close cousin was the "emergent strategy" school, which proposed that good ideas would emerge from the muddling and that those should be followed.

Then the mathematicians got into the game and noted that strategies had to build off game theory: Competitors will take account of each other's likely actions, and reactions to actions, in calculating their own. The timing was good for this idea because game theory generally assumes that perfect information is available to the players; secrets spoil the game. The Internet, of course, has come along to provide just the sort of pricing and resource transparency that Nash equilibrium theories require. But even game theory assumes that players can fully evaluate the relevant data and make predictions about the future. It doesn't explain what to do when both sides have too much information and too little time to evaluate it, which are precisely the conditions of chess and today's business world.

People management is usually considered a separate topic from strategy. Of course, it isn't: Plans cannot succeed without the right people to implement them, learning organizations won't learn if they don't have any students inside, and emergent strategies won't emerge if the right folks aren't detecting and fostering them. All organizations are composed of people of different abilities and motives, and despite what the HR folks say, the way people act does not change much regardless of what job title you bestow, how much training you provide, or what the job description says. So yet another important element of success is the art of "strategic people management": creating structures for these relatively inflexible "pieces" to best perform the desired tasks.

I guess you can see where this is headed.

The argument of this book is that chess is a physical manifestation of just about all the ideas that the authors and academics have been arguing about. It is, in fact, a centuries-old test bed for these key concepts, its players lab rats trying out the best strategies for conducting a competition of organizations composed of pieces with different skill sets and values in a rapidly changing environment.

To test the proposition, let's revisit those three big waves of strategy studies. Certainly any good player is skilled at choosing what squares (markets or industries) he is setting forth to control, just as executives were taught to seek out the most profitable ones. Players are equally expert in knowing how to coordinate the actions of their different pieces, to create efficient and well-run organizations: to "compete on capabilities." Finally, they have developed highly refined techniques for using those strengths against particular weak spots in the opponent's position: to "compete on resources."

Players' strategies do emerge over time; they are the very subjects of game theory, and their plans are based on "strategic HR."

Finally, as befits the information age business, a Grandmaster is under immense time pressure that requires decisions to be made "too quickly." He understands very well that he cannot see the future clearly but that he must nonetheless make decisions and chart a plan anyway.

Of course, chess is not a perfect representation of the business world. First and most important, it permits only one winner and assumes only one opponent. Second, it provides equal starting resources, an orderly taking of turns, and that both players agree on and follow the same set of rules. Third, as noted, there are no lies and no secrets in the chess world. Finally, but very importantly from this book's point of view, it is far, far simpler than the business world.

For as mammothly complex as chess is, as unimaginable as all the possibilities are, it is still a game played with just six different kinds of pieces on a board measuring eight squares by eight squares. How does that compare with the complexity of life? How does having a single opponent, playing under strict rule, with equal resources and clear time limitations, compare with the jungle of modern-day business competition?

The point is that both pursuits involve fighting for success in an unknowable future. The fact that one is even more unknowable than the other doesn't matter: In both, you have to move when you can't be sure how to proceed.

OK, but how far ahead *do* great players look? One of the strongest GMs in history, Richard Reti, answered this question as follows: "One move."

What he was really saying was that, for the bulk of moves in a game, there is no clear expectation of a certain line of play. Consider a human-versus-computers matchup. Humans do beat the machines but never by seeing some amazing combination that the computer missed six moves out, catching the silicon beast off guard and surprising it with a checkmate. Given the disparity of computing power, that just doesn't happen. Instead, people can succeed by playing "positional" chess, accumulating small advantages in minibattles, all conducted in the furtherance of a *general* overall strategic plan, which plan itself is subject to constant revision. By limiting the focus to thematically linked, small-stakes battles, minor advantages can be accumulated into a winning position.

That's the essence of why Kasparov can still compete with Deep Blue: he isn't trying to think through every possible response, response to the response, and so on. He simply can't, but because of the complexity of the game, neither can the computer (although it, on the other hand, does try).

Instead, to compete amid such incomprehensible complexity, GMs rely on a set of strategies and techniques developed over hundreds of years of experience. These principles have direct business analogues. That is very understandable, because they boil down to methods of conducting a contest between organizations of players of different abilities and values when there are too many possibilities to know exactly what the best possible move is. Those ideas are the subject of this book.

As you learn these techniques, you will see that a great player's decision-making process does indeed require cogitation and discipline. It's not so easy to intelligently short-circuit the need to look at a few billion positions and come up with the right answer! But if you do make the effort, at your next cocktail party, in answer to several questions on the subject from your admiring public, maybe you'll be able to explain that the reason you've been so successful is that you've learned to see three moves ahead.

You needn't explain that it's just a question of *which* three.

* * *

Maybe you'd like a better idea of exactly what you're getting into here, so here's an overview.

"First Mover" (Chapter 3) provides chess lessons for the beginning stages of any venture, whether launched in a garage or born in a boardroom. "On the Clock" (Chapter 4) illustrates the need to iterate rapidly rather than trying to devise a perfect plan. "Bad Bishops" (Chapter 5) shows how executives can build the most effective possible organizations with their executive pieces and knowledge workers.

Next up is Chapter 6, "Lucky or Good?" which addresses the basic question of what plans are, how to make them, and when to change them. There follow Chapters 7, 8, and 9, a tour of some of the most effective basic chess ideas for executives: "Strong Squares," "Sac the Exchange!" and a host of others in "Classic Tactics." With all that information, you should have several good options on any move, and "Decisions, Decisions" (Chapter 10) shows how to choose among them (quickly! you're still "on the clock"). Finally, there's one last lesson, a review of the previous ones, in "A Postgame Recap."

At the end, I hope you'll agree with me that the principles derived from a millennium of chess play provide wonderful models for prospering in the most uncertain business times in history.

CHAPTER THREE

FIRST
MOVER

The problems facing a chess player at the starting position and those facing any businessperson considering a new venture are very similar. New enterprises, whether launched inside a large organization or a small garage, face fundamentally different sorts of questions than do established businesses. Entrepreneurs and intrapreneurs have to worry about what market to attack, how to develop a team, and how to "get in the game" quickly and effectively. These are exactly the issues a player faces at the beginning of a chess game.

You probably know that chess players do not start by just mindlessly pushing the wood around until something interesting begins to happen. They begin the game by playing an "opening," a pattern of moves that has a clear overarching idea, a theme that will dictate the course of the game. The opening you play dictates how much risk to take, how rapid the development must be, and the order in which the members of your team are brought out; in short, it generally sets up the organization and its goals.

There is an opening for every taste and style. A standard general work on the subject, the *Modern Chess Openings*,[1] runs to more than 800 pages, and that covers just overviews of the major ones. Some emulate guerilla warfare, sniping at the opponent from the corners and wings; some, like the "Spanish Torture," grind an opponent down with an excruciatingly slow buildup of pressure.

Fans of Jim Collins's *From Good to Great* (Collins, 2001) will be interested to know that there is even a "Hedgehog" opening that beautifully mirrors his "hedgehog principle" of tenacious focus on existing turf.

Despite their vast variation, however, chess openings can be categorized, as biologists do the species of life, into a handful of major groups. These groups, in turn, reflect very different approaches to battle, differences that closely mirror the few basic business models available to entrepreneurs. As you would expect, each family of openings offers certain key lessons for enterprises using the analogous business model. So, at the end of this chapter, I'll propose an "opening repertoire" for new venturists.

FIRST-MOVER ADVANTAGE

The goal of a chess or business opening is to create a difference you can exploit later in the game. That's it. Now, it's become common wisdom that companies with the "first-mover advantage" have a huge edge in entering a market. But is that always true? Let's see how it works in the game that gave birth to the term.

White always gets the first move, and statistically, it is indeed a significant edge. When equally strong players square off, White wins about 40 percent more games than Black. On the other hand, if it's such an advantage, how come the best players don't always win with White? Because, as in business, it's all a question of how this putative advantage is used. If it is exploited to create that difference we're looking for out of the opening, great; but it's easy to waste or misplay it entirely. As we'll see in later chapters, simply gaining an advantage out of the opening hardly guarantees a win in either pursuit.

In general, the first-mover advantage is potentially present anytime a new product or service is introduced to the public. For our purposes, we're going to say that companies doing this are playing White: They are making the first move. Companies that enter an existing market, by contrast, are playing Black: Someone has moved ahead of them. (We will discuss opening ideas for Black later in the chapter.)

eBay, Skype, YouTube, and TripAdvisor certainly attest to the fact that first-mover advantage can result in massive success. Conversely, many entrepreneurs and investors wave the first-mover flag on entering the fray, invoking its divine protection, only to find out, like members of the Children's Crusade, that they were merely to become optimistic martyrs. Segway, the maker of the breakthrough personal locomotion device, was certainly a first mover in every sense but an economic disappointment nonetheless.

The key to understanding the first-mover advantage and how to use it is to appreciate the two basic varieties of the beast: network effect and classic. It's important to know the difference because thinking you have one variety and playing it that way, only to find out that you actually had the other, is usually fatal.

If an opportunity exists to leverage a network effect before anyone else does, riskier play is justified because the attendant advantages are so enormous (and because, if anyone beats you to it, you'll lose). Congratulations, you get to play the "King's Gambit," and we'll show you how in a few pages.

But most businesses launching new products or services do not really have that opportunity, even if a network, like the Internet, is somehow involved. For those companies, the classic first mover is the relevant concept, and that requires a different sort of play altogether. A "Ruy Lopez," explained in a bit, is more for you.

METCALFE'S LAW, USED AND ABUSED

The term *first-mover advantage* has been around a long time but only became popular business jargon in the nineties, after the introduction of "Metcalfe's Law." This describes how the value of networks increases rapidly with additional users and how such networks could effectively preempt competition.

Bob Metcalfe, the pioneer of Ethernet technology that drove the first computer networks, thought of it as a way of explaining why firms should bother to adopt his relatively expensive technology. His law says that the value of a network increases proportionately with the square of the number of its users. Thus, although it might not make sense to purchase networking equipment for just a few users, the positive impact of having lots of users far outweighs the total cost of the required network cards (because benefits would improve quadratically while costs only increase linearly). Well, you at least have to admit he's the smartest sales guy you ever heard of.

The basic idea is certainly right enough in a number of cases. A simple example is fax machines. If only two people have them, neither is very valuable, but the value of each rises dramatically as more people buy them.

eBay is perhaps the most profitable application of the law. Like fax machine users, each new member was a potential recipient and contributor, both a potential buyer and a potential seller. Whether you want to auction something off or find a unique item, you want to be part of the biggest possible community. Thus, size begets size and a near monopoly. That's the real network-effect first mover.

A less-well-known but extremely important example was Kaazaa, the music-sharing software perhaps most directly responsible for the downfall of the music industry's business model. Like eBay, each new member both took from the system and contributed to it, creating a true network effect. Because you want to have access to the largest virtual library of songs, an early lead in the number of users became wildly self-reinforcing. This lesson was not lost on the founders, who went on to create the biggest free voice-over Internet protocol (VOIP) system, Skype, and now are finishing their Internet tear through existing media industries with Joost, an attack on television networks and cable operators.

A slightly different application of the idea explains why Windows and VHS became industry standards. Once enough people adopt a specific technical standard in a new industry, the content makers begin to develop to that standard, which means more consumers will adopt it and more companies will make content for it. Microsoft won personal computer World War I because it opened its operating system to outside developers. As a result, many more applications became available for Windows PCs than for Macs, which made those computers more useful. So, naturally, more people bought them, which drove more developers to create applications for them, which meant more buyers, and so on. Again, the beautiful thing about capturing a network effect like this is that it can overwhelm competition. The problem is how often it is trotted out for cases that sound plausible but don't really fit.

For example, the first-mover advantage was the basis of the argument for Webvan, Etoys, Pets.com, and other bubble disasters. But these, like most Web retailing sites, were not really subject to the law: *The buyers of normal commercial products are really not part of a network because they contribute nothing back to it* aside from a marginal buying power advantage, certainly nothing close to a squaring of *n* plus 1. Thus, despite the fact that it operates on the Internet, Amazon is not a beneficiary of the network effect (although it did benefit from the classic first-mover advantage described later).

Poor Mr. Metcalfe's law was ideal for abuse by investment banks during the bubble because they could use it as genuine scientific proof that throwing insane amounts of money at any concept was a good idea. Of course, the Internet had to be involved somehow—that was the required network—which was perfect because it explained why such an investment philosophy had not previously been smart. When uttered by the bankers, in fact, the words typically implied that further questions would indicate a rather painful naïveté. To simplify matters, their rallying cry became "GBQ": "get big quick"—less elegant, perhaps, but more to the point.

Webvan was the classic GBQ company. Armed with that philosophy and a basically good idea, it went from IPO to Chapter 11 in just two years (not surprisingly, almost exactly the same life span as Etoys and many others). Its approach to home delivery of groceries was to invest vast sums of money into planned 26 food distribution centers, each with a stupefying capacity equal to the output of 18 traditional grocery stores. Given the known thin margins in food retailing, such size was required to make the deal attractive; the flip side was that unless utilization of the centers was extremely high, the whole enterprise would be a Hindenburg. It wasn't, so it was.

On the other hand, the same idea—but with a measured tempo instead of a frantic one—has been employed successfully by

FreshDirect, which attacked the market in a much more focused, low-risk way. It built one distribution center in a geographic location, New York City, where grocery delivery is a more attractive option than it is elsewhere. By iterating constantly, it has refined the business model and product mix to a point that it has reached profitability with 250,000 customers and $150 million in sales.[2] Webvan is an example of the false allure of first-mover advantage. FreshDirect shows that playing Black can be just fine.

More illustrative still of how rarely the real network effect "opportunity bird" is sighted is the case of SunRocket, the first company to seriously attempt commercialization of VOIP. Despite its early entry and the fact that users of VOIP are obviously part of a network (and one that expands in value with users), no network effect was available for capture because the technology was standard and easily replicable: Any company's customers could call any other's. Collectively, there was indeed a network effect, but without proprietary standards to enforce, that value was spread widely among all entrants. A well-funded start-up, by 2007 SunRocket had become perhaps the first significant telecommunications company in U.S. history to suddenly cease operations and leave its users in the lurch. A noteworthy milestone, but not exactly the first that investors expected.

As SunRocket illustrates, then, even when the network effect first-mover advantage is present, it is often unclear how investors can extract the "value" created by the network in question. For every eBay, which actually produces earnings, there are countless Friendsters struggling for ways to generate cash from their highly useful but business-model-less networks—that is, aside from another Wall Street favorite, the "greater fool theory," which somehow seems to work often enough but is outside the scope of this book.

CLASSIC FIRST MOVER

Fortunately, there is a more common species of the first-mover effect that is also real, if somewhat less powerful. If the network effect does not explain the fact that White wins most games, what does? It's simply that, with the first move, White gets the biggest say in the overall pattern the game will take. It is not so much that White has an insurmountable lead in getting its forces into the field and will therefore necessarily win. Rather, it's that White is dictating the direction of the game. Black has to react to White's pattern of deployment, but White gets to take that reaction into account, reformulate the plan, and again push Black to respond. White essentially determines the architecture of the game and, with sharp play, can dictate its direction and tempo for some time. Black isn't helpless; it can try to seize the initiative but usually only by incurring risks that exceed the tolerance of most players. In general, White keeps a half-move advantage (until a tempo is wasted; see Chapter 4, "On the Clock") and is therefore a step ahead using the feedback loop created by the game's alternating moves.

This version of first mover is a powerful business advantage if, along with the new product or service, the mover (1) creates a feedback loop that generates a "knowledge lead" over new market entrants, and (2) that lead is used to iterate faster and hence dictate the action. Otherwise, first just means first, and companies that go first might well miss the best target market, or get that part right but the exact implementation wrong. Being approximately correct, by itself, just shows competition what not to do.

It's really all about who uses the resulting feedback loop better and faster, and that is certainly not always White. After all, Google was a second mover: Overture, now part of Yahoo!, brought the paid-search business model to market, but it was Google that saw how to perfect it.

Indeed, there is an easy way to see that first-mover advantage is in the feedback loop: Most victorious entrepreneurs report that the basic model they initially pursued was *not* ultimately the source of the company's success.[3] As they moved, new wrinkles became apparent, but because of the active use of the first-mover advantage, they kept discovering and exploiting these before the competition. Over time, the businesses became something different from what was originally envisioned, although the core idea of the enterprise remained. Once again, it is not a question of seeing the future with certainty, of having a fixed plan many moves out; it's a matter of moving in accordance with an overall idea but actively adjusting as the feedback loop dictates. That's how the first-mover advantage creates what we want out of the opening and then keeps it alive.

A CLASSIC FIRST MOVER

Email Data Source, Inc., a young company in New York, had this idea: "competitive intelligence" for e-mail marketing. So, for example, Land's End might check out what e-mails Eddie Bauer sent to its customers last Father's Day and what the impact was so they'll have a better idea how to compete this selling season. This sort of thing is popular in other marketing media, like television spots, Internet ads, and even direct mail; everybody wants to know what their competitors are doing and how effective they are with it.

It made big-picture sense that there'd be a market for the concept, but no network effect would be present, nor could any meaningful intellectual property barriers be established. Thus, any traction would bring imitators, and success or failure would depend on the classic first-mover advantage.

Email Data Source began by creating "seed" accounts, fictitious customers who would receive e-mail from every marketer they could find. When the e-mails started showing up, the company compiled them into a large database.

This immediately created a first-mover advantage, not because they had the e-mails, but because they began to see what the real questions were. For example, how do you structure the database? How do you provide customers with easy access to the information they want? How do you scale the seed account creation process, with different IDs and return e-mail addresses, and still track their origin? Of course, these were just the first questions. There were others: Which demographic groups should the seed accounts represent (because companies send different pitches to different groups)? Most important by far, which companies would buy the service and on what terms?

There was no way to know the answers to these questions without getting out there and moving, trying things, adjusting, and trying again. And the knowledge gained from this trial-error-and-retrial process is the essence of the first-mover advantage. Every bit of insight they gained and plowed back into the system increased the distance between them and a later entrant.

The initial users of the system were not at all what the company expected. Brand managers turned out not to be the early customers. Instead, having access to "who's sending what e-mail to whom and how" actually was most valuable for other e-mail industry participants, companies that wanted to buy and sell e-mail lists, handle distribution of mass e-mails, and the like. It turns out that this group was dying for information about its own industry. Another surprise was that the second-most-aggressive early adopters were folks in the online casino industry. Because this group suffered such severe limitations on how else they could market themselves, their lifeblood was solicitation by e-mail, so they had more incentive than other groups to give the system a try.

In fact, it turned out that the basic business model did not work for the customers for which it was intended. The one-size-fits-all pricing was a little rich for individual brand managers and at the same time gave them more than they wanted; they really just wanted to know about a few competing brands, not every company in the database. As a result, the sales targets were pushing the decision up to corporate, which would try to get several other groups interested and split the cost. Naturally, that slowed the sales cycle and prevented any real momentum for a young company that desperately needed it to impress prospective investors.

But, again, the company successfully applied the advantages of being a first mover. It changed its model and product, bringing the per-brand price down and limiting users' access to information about specific competitors. That worked much better. And, given the lower sales price and more targeted user set, the new model also made the product ideal for channel resellers, like advertising agencies and e-mail service providers, that could fold the cost of the service into the fees paid by their customers. Bingo: The previously unseen channel opportunities keyed a sales explosion.

Of course, every financial projection in all of the early budgets turned out to be completely wrong, as did the staffing projections, product plans, target industry segments, and basic business model. But none of that mattered because they properly exploited the first-mover advantage.

By the way, these typical wild variances from plan are of special import for intrapreneurs, those brave souls who attempt to launch new ventures inside large companies. The lesson is that they are always better off in a separate organization from the established company. No matter how much the "mother ship" protests that it doesn't care, the inability to hit numbers, dates, and plans will drive traditional managers insane; it's much better to be totally outside the big company's processes. Using the same structures to govern both kinds of enterprises would be as much of a train wreck as having the biggest government in the world trying to run a small municipality just because they're co-located in the same . . . oops, never mind.

YAHOO!'S OPENING

A slightly better-known example is Yahoo! How did it start? With Jerry Yang and David Filo—two guys in a trailer on the Stanford campus. Their earth-shattering idea was to record their favorite sites on the newly born Internet so other people could find and enjoy them, too. Well, it didn't exactly sound like a blueprint for one of the most successful companies of the decade, but the first-mover advantage took care of that.

The advantage was at work from the moment they faced their most basic question: What was the best way to keep track of all these sites and make them easy for someone else to find? Funny as it seems, the answer was incredibly retro: by categories and, when the categories got too big, by subcategories—a Dewey decimal system, for those of you old enough to remember paper-based libraries. This simple idea was much handier than a huge searchable database, the "natural" way to organize digital data.

Armed with this crucial first-mover advantage, the system took off, with lots of friends and friends of friends making contributions and then checking out the sites other people had located. Eventually, they opened the collection to the public, along with a "Cool Site of the Day" feature, as "Jerry and David's Guide to the World Wide Web."

That was in 1994. Word of mouth among the cognoscenti drove increasing user traffic, and Sequoia Capital funded them with $2 million a year later.

The first-mover advantage kept paying dividends because, as online usage grew, the need for help finding things on the Web exploded. Eventually the Yahoo! site became so useful as a guide to the Internet jungle that people started to set it as their home page, the most logical place to begin any Internet session. (This idea of a "home page" had not existed just a couple of years earlier. Indeed, Netscape blew an opportunity to maintain its temporary Internet dominance by failing to recognize the benefit of having everyone start their online sessions on its site, which accidentally happened by default in the heyday of Navigator: In this way, they utterly fumbled their own first-mover advantage.)

Having first moved its way into this much Internet traffic, the economics kicked in when Internet advertising finally took off after a couple of false starts. Because Yahoo! already had the traffic and could see how people responded to ads, the company had an incredible advantage in this area. Moreover, once the idea that keeping the users on the site (rather than sending them away because they'd clicked on an ad) became obvious, Yahoo! again had a big advantage. It already knew enough about the habits and desires of its users to provide the most popular content on its own pages: It "knew" what content would be successful and so began to keep users on the site and to drive advertising revenues even higher. Yahoo!'s first-mover knowledge advantage constantly set the stage for making good next moves as the Web matured.

Today, that company that Sequoia bought a big chunk of for $2 million in 1994 is worth about $40 billion. (No wonder VCs have a skewed sense of risk and reward—but that's another story.)

What the stories of Email Data Source and Yahoo! demonstrate is the value of being the classic first mover: having the ability to *shape the game,* to get and keep a knowledge and know-how advantage through constant iteration. Being the first mover is an advantage only if you incorporate the resulting learning into your products and business models fast enough that you stay ahead of the competition; if you don't, it's a disadvantage because you become the road map that shows competitors what not to do when they come after you. Let's observe a moment of silence for Kaypro, Wang, and Commodore, first movers of the PC industry.

WHAT'S THE BIG IDEA?

"What's the big idea?" one of my Grandmaster friends always asked when he walked up to a board and surveyed the scene. And he meant it. He wanted to know, in a few words, what each side was trying to accomplish. What is White's "elevator pitch?" How about Black's? It's this fundamental battle of ideas, rather than a detailed if-then move analysis, that average fans enjoy. (Think about watching a football play: The fun is in guessing whether the defense will blitz Payton Manning and how he'll adjust the play in response, not in exactly how the up-front blocking assignments work.)

Odd as it may seem to the uninitiated, good chess players can always tell you their elevator pitch; they can sum up their basic battle plan in a few words. Odd as it is to the fully initiated, many executives can't. But they sure can lay a big fat business plan on you.

BUSINESS PLANS

Sophisticated business plans have long been considered the corporate equivalent of a high school diploma: an essential ingredient of success. Indeed, an entire industry has sprung up to "help" young businesses put their plans together, and legions of consultants do the same for established companies looking at diversifying into new areas. The New York Angels, maybe the leading early-stage investment consortium in the country, sees hundreds of these plans each month. Many of them are impressive, like doctoral theses: chockful of deep competitive analysis, multiyear sales forecasts, and long-term product plans.

Of course, says David S. Rose, the founding Angel, they are also inevitably totally wrong. For new ventures (and these days, even well-established ones), there are simply too many unknowns. What company can seriously defend sales projections down to the tens of thousands of dollars three years out? Forecasting sales three *months* out is more of a challenge than most can handle.

Projections come in two basic varieties: top down, and bottom up. They bring different fallacies to the table.

Top Down

Rose points out that the top-down forecasting method is usually based on some variation of the following proposition. We want to start a company to make gloves. There are 1.3 billion Chinese and thus 2.6 billion naked hands there. If we sell *to only 1 percent* of them at just $5 per hand, we'll make over $100 million! Indeed.

As good as this example is, though, it's recently been trumped by none other than Kraft Foods, showing that such silliness is by no means confined to inexperienced entrepreneurs. Turns out that sales of cheese are down and Kraft is worried. A study alarmingly found that peanut butter and jelly sandwiches (at 3.7 billion per year) had overtaken grilled cheese sandwiches (at a mere 2.2 billion) as the third-favorite lunch sandwich. Apparently, Kraft then hired the strategist from the Chinese gloves company, for they now project big revenue increases on converting *just a fraction* of those "peanut butter moms." Of course, the fact that grilled cheese doesn't exactly work as pre-prepared lunch (almost certainly the real problem) is ignored in this kind of "analysis."

So beware forecasts of great success based on just a tiny fraction of an enormous market: It all sounds so very reasonable, but you still have to show how you're going to get there.

Bottoms Up

Here, the attraction is the opposite. The pitch is built from the ground up, based on lots of data about historical trends, spreadsheets full of raw numbers, and precise projections. The most dangerously seductive ones are based on highly analogous circumstances. These "feel right" because the baseline data are real and known. But they still must be adjusted for a broad range of human behaviors and responses, no matter how similar the situations appear.

Again, to use a big company example to avoid casting aspersions on the innocent, consider Euro Disney. Here was a project for which tons of (apparently) highly analogous data were available to the planners: how many people might come for how long, what they'd pay, and what they'd consume. It's hard to think of a case where the data being analyzed could have been more relevant. In practice, however, all the projections turned out to be drastically wrong. Cultural differences like fast food preferences were not adequately considered (oddly, the image damage from this faux pas was largely repaired by a spokesrodent replacement: the gourmet rat Remy for a food-clueless Mickey). As usual, small errors in key assumptions like restaurant usage and length of overnight stays quickly compounded into severely different actual results.

Just about the only way these kinds of projections turn out to be close to right is when huge offsetting errors are serendipitously built in. So, while this kind of analysis can seem persuasive, it is helpful to remember the other activity in which the name of this approach is frequently invoked.

THE IDEA BEHIND THE BUSINESS PLAN

Given the above, it's become fashionable to ask if business plans really are helpful. One academic study concluded no: Based on an analysis of successful companies, it found little difference between those that had a plan and those that didn't. This reeks of the same logical flaw that permeates many business books: If you don't consider failed companies in the sample, you're missing a large part of the truth.

And, sure enough, it turns out that, of failed businesses, a greater proportion didn't have a plan than did. Hence, in the aggregate, a substantially greater percentage of companies with plans survive than do those without them.

So if detailed plans are always wrong, but lack of a plan is a problem, what sort of plan should a company have? Chess gives us the answer.

The Chess Guide to Business Plans

We already mentioned the incredibly intimidating *Modern Chess Openings*. Just picking it up could put one off chess for the rest of one's life. Instead, the book we mere mortals need was written about 50 years ago by Ruben Fine and is called *The Ideas Behind the Chess Openings* (Bell, 1959). The author's point is that you do not need to memorize the few thousand lines of an opening such as the "Sicilian Dragon" to play it well, but you do need to understand what the basic points of the opening are and pursue those goals as the game progresses through the early stages.

To give players a better sense of what we mean, we'll descibe those key points here; but if you don't play just know these are the most basic building blocks of the strategy and skip to the next paragraph. What a Dragon player aims for is to "fianchetto" his King's Bishop immediately to take control of the board's long diagonal; open the c-file and put his Rook on it; and, longer term, look to make trouble for White on the Queen's side of the board by coordinating the action of that Bishop and that Rook. If the player plugs away at achieving these aims and follows a few commonsense rules (mentioned below), he'll usually get a perfectly adequate game to play.

And that's exactly the situation with business plans. What most companies really need is not so much a highly detailed business blueprint but, rather, a clear expression of "the idea behind the business plan." Business plans should set the direction, establish patterns of deployment, and dictate risk-taking parameters and investment limits. But they should always have built-in flexibility, be opportunistic, and include only as much detailed planning as is absolutely necessary.

Thus, a business plan should contain *simple* descriptions of these few points: (1) the product or service you plan to offer and how it differs from existing ones, (2) the barriers to entry you'll erect, (3) an order-of-magnitude guess about the size of the market you're targeting, (4) the executive team, (5) a go-to-market plan, (6) a revenue model that describes how you'll get paid, and (7) an overall financial model for the business. If you're an entrepreneur seeking outside capital, you should also describe possible "exit strategies" that will allow investors to get their money back. These core points constitute the Big Idea that should drive the business.

So does all this mean that a business plan should be more like a mission statement? A chess organization's mission statement concocted by a modern business consultant might go: "To be the leading provider of spatial control, midgame tactics, and endgame brilliancies; to offer meaningful and satisfying enrichment opportunities to our pawns, minor pieces, and other members of our community; and to generate spectator value for our kibitzers, tournament directors, and the chess world at large." Uh, OK, fine, but where do my pieces go?

Forget these things; they're about what you want to *be* (and they're usually silly and overblown to boot). What you need to know is, what do you want to *do*? That tells you where to position your pieces, what their jobs are, how they need to support each other, and in what order to develop them.

OPENING PRINCIPLES

In the opening phases of both chess and business, the Big Idea should always be kept in mind while following these simple rules.

Develop the Team

Novice players typically get their Queens out early and spend their moves having her chase around enemy pieces. With a little experience, the player learns how to use the Queen in combination with another piece or two, usually a Bishop, and to play for an early checkmate.

The problem with this sort of all-or-nothing approach is simple: If it doesn't work (which it certainly shouldn't), the entire rest of his army is undeveloped. There is no plan B, and his undeveloped pieces are ripe for an attack by the fully deployed enemy force.

We often see this problem at the New York Angels: a company takes its immature idea out to market too early, before developing the team or infrastructure to support it. The company doesn't have the mechanisms or people in place to absorb and process the market feedback (again, the key to the classic first-mover advantage), and it certainly cannot handle raising money, finding customers, creating infrastructure, and the other key tasks with the limited group it has. The result is usually an early flameout.

Instead, at the start of the game, a chess player thinks almost exclusively about developing the entire team as rapidly as possible. Good players try to spend just one move on each piece until they've all been moved out of their starting positions. (Pawn moves, in particular, are kept to an absolute minimum, just enough to allow the pieces behind them to escape the back row.) Everything else comes later. Emmanuel Lasker, the longest-reigning world champion in history, used to say that if your pieces are developed properly, "the combinations will come as naturally as a baby's smile."

Similarly, in building a successful venture, the team must be built before the market attack is initiated. Countless enterprises have failed for lack of getting good people into the right jobs early enough, and, indeed, many venture capitalists are more interested in the quality of the team than the exact proposal for which it seeks funding. Because entrepreneurs tend to be terrible at defining jobs and delegating authority, they commonly fail to recruit a full team or to put players into positions with the maximum positive impact on the organization's success. We'll see more about this in Chapter Five, "Bad Bishops."

Castle Early: Create Barriers to Entry

Good players always castle early in the game, getting their King to relative safety in the corner of the board surrounded by defenders. Leaving your King unprotected in the middle of the board is certain disaster.

Weirdly, this also is a mistake many beginning companies make. No matter how profound the breakthrough, you can't leave it unprotected. Think about TiVo and Netscape, two companies that changed the world with little to show for it.

Protection can come in many forms: Patents regarding the key intellectual property can be powerful deterrents, of course, but so can exclusive contracts with key suppliers or distributors; sewing up the rights to use well-known brand names; or a lock on key industry talent (make sure to get your non-competition agreements in place so they can't wander off to work for competitors). Of course, a true network-effect first-mover advantage can itself be protection.

Although the information age has destroyed a number of traditional business barriers, it has also created a new one: a great URL. Weather.com, for example, has a permanent advantage in its industry. The raw value of the right URL is best evidenced by Business.com, the rights to which were purchased for $7 million in 1999 to howls of derision . . . which turned to sighs of envy when the property was auctioned for over $300 million in 2007. In the interim, the domain owners had simply acted as a directory site for business services, getting compensated for the referrals of people who figured it was a natural place to start a search for an accounting firm or office supplies.

At the end of the day, "barrier" is too strong a word for these defensive works; "impediment" is about all you can really hope for. By far the best defense in the information age is speed of iteration, as discussed in later chapters. But it's still a good idea to make your competitors navigate an obstacle course while they're trying to chase you down.

It's also important to remember who you're barring the door against. One of my favorite recurring scenes in venture capital meetings happens when the VC asks the aspiring Internet mogul: "Well, yes, that is a good idea, but why couldn't Google do it?" (it's a telltale sign of my age that in my own start-up days, the question featured Microsoft). This is usually followed by an extremely entertaining explanation of all the reasons that Google couldn't possibly get to market faster and better than this little start-up. Well, regardless of what that big new idea is, or what the intellectual property protections are, or how much of a genius your CTO is, the answer is . . . *of course* Google could enter the market! It could crush you like a bug! But, it *could* choose to enter the cement business, too. My guess is that it won't. Like any large company, Google has its hands full of major issues, with its resources dedicated along specific business lines. It's focused on its big competitors and large future markets. It simply doesn't care about that $50 million of revenue you'll produce a few years out. If, indeed, you get the business going and it turns out to be strategically relevant to Google's world, it might buy you, but it's not going to worry about trying to compete you out of business.

Don't Play for Fool's Mate

"Fool's Mate" is a way Black can win the game on his second move. Unfortunately, unless White happens to start with exactly the two right moves, it doesn't work. It's certainly an unsound plan for the game, but many beginners hope for it anyway.

So do many entrepreneurs, looking for similarly lucky results. For a year after News Corp. bought MySpace for $580 million, the New York Angels were swamped by business plans consisting of two parts: the size of some potential social network and the mind-boggling price Rupert Murdoch paid for a money-losing site. The implication was that any vaguely similar business had similar prospects, regardless of a lack of novel technology or any kind of revenue model. It's like having a little elderly lady walk in the door and say, "Yesterday, the lotto was hit by an old woman who was wearing a red dress when she bought the ticket. If you give me $10, I'll put on my red dress, buy one, and we'll split the winnings." Silly, but far more reasonable than investing in efforts to become MySpace II: It'll cost much less.

Setting out to replicate such stories is playing for fool's mate. Both *could* work; both are fundamentally unsound. Instead, try one of the more serious openings described next.

AN ENTREPRENEURIAL REPERTOIRE

So, what opening should you play? It depends on the sort of venture you're trying to launch, of course (and on your own stomach). But the following repertoire of openings might prove useful.

First you have to know which color you're playing. New ventures can generally be divided into two major categories: those in which a brand-new market is being pursued, and those in which a new idea is being launched into an existing market. The first set can be seen as situations in which the new venture is "playing White": moving first into new territory. In the second category, somebody else has gone first; you're playing Black, contesting a previous entrant.

OPENINGS FOR WHITE

When you're targeting a new market, you must move quickly for the simple reason that you can bet that others have the same idea you do and are also pursuing it. We see this constantly at the Angels, and every VC I know says the same thing: Once somebody shows up with a good idea, you'll see several more permutations of the same theme in the next few months. So, as we'll discuss in Chapter 4 ("On the Clock"), you can waste neither clock time nor tempo time. You've got to go!

Still, the question is, How fast is fast? Do we throw caution to the winds and hemorrhage money to obtain growth, or simply grow as quickly as possible while being fiscally cautious? To me, the answer is, If there's a genuine network-effect opportunity, it's time for the first option, a King's Gambit; otherwise, first movers should play the more traditional Ruy Lopez.

The King's Gambit

The King's Gambit is one of the most famous of the swashbuckling, gambling, free-for-all openings that became the rage during the "Romantic" period in chess history, when—it's no coincidence—the Three Musketeers were cultural icons. In those days, it was considered "unmanly" to play a game without offering a pawn or two to open attacking lines and bad manners not to accept the sacrifices and then try to heroically fend off the ensuing blitzkrieg.

The great "gambiteers" would have no tolerance for the namby-pamby, risk-adverse openings that came to dominate the chess scene in the 1950s and 1960s (it took Michael Tal, Bobby Fischer, and then Garry Kasparov to reawaken these wonderful old attacking systems). And now that we're going through a "romantic period" of business, when great fortunes are created from nothing other than some computer code and a Web connection, they seem relevant again.

It's a blast to play these openings in business and chess because they allow you to do what diet pitches promise: Be utterly irresponsible without feeling guilty! You can press the attack regardless of the cost. In chess, *cost* means the loss of material or the creation of other permanent weaknesses. If the game goes on for a long time, these will be fatal. But the idea is to get to checkmate long before that matters. Unfortunately, in business, *cost* means cost, so you need some understanding backers if you are going to play this way.

Trying to figure out whether you really have a network-effect opportunity is tricky. The question is, are we winning market share or just plain "share" without a market? Lots of business gambiteers have fired up what they thought was a "mating net" around a network-effect opportunity, only to find out that there was no way to either get to checkmate or to recover their large material losses. For example, remember Cosmo 3D? Probably not. Well, the good news was that the hundreds of millions of dollars invested over several years by Silicon Graphics and others did produce something like a standard for interactive 3D graphics; the bad news was that 3D did not turn out to be an industry.

But if you decide that the network effect is there and play the King's Gambit, it's really kind of simple. You open lines and attack as fast as possible, regardless of the material cost, and throw everything you've got at creating the standard. Even our usual "develop the whole team" rules don't always apply. In such an opening, overemphasizing engineering or marketing (depending on what type of network you're after) can work.

YouTube was a classic example. They were certainly sacrificing material left and right, with massive losses coming from the huge infrastructure costs of uploading, storing, handling, and downloading all those videos. They couldn't, and still can't, point to a meaningful business model. It was all a marketing attack: a brilliant way of leveraging MySpace users into a network-effect first-mover advantage that Google took to mean "game over" and, so, bought it. Meantime, more "sensible" players in the space, like Brightcove, were taking the time to develop their team, a good business model, and great technology tools. But it was checkmate long before these long-term benefits could pay off.

Just remember: *There is no turning back in a gambit opening.* You can't get cold feet 15 moves into the game, when you're already down a piece, and suddenly decide to husband resources. If you're playing a gambit, you're playing a gambit, and the only thing that matters is opening more lines to the opponent's King. Win, or die gloriously. YouTube could not have switched to a more economically sensible model (like Brightcove had) once its user acquisition strategy gained steam; there was no way to change its money-losing course and remain relevant.

Therefore, all your high-risk decisions about functions and product specifications (by definition, those making predictions about incredibly uncertain markets) have to be right the first time. Even when you get the industry right, you can get the standard wrong.

No doubt, the most famous example of the perils of fighting for a network first-mover advantage—even when one has correctly identified a game where that might be the right strategy—is the VHS-Betamax battle. This qualifies as a network-effect race of the industry-standard variety: The more consumers who had a particular product, the more content would be made for that standard, which would drive more consumers to it, and so on.

Sony raced to market well ahead of the pack with its Betamax VCRs and, by all accounts, the quality of the recordings was fine. But they didn't win for a type of reason that is easy to see with hindsight but was nearly impossible to see beforehand. In the VCR world, this happened to be maximum permissible recording time.

As it turned out, the main early use was to record movies, which required at least a two-hour recording period. Betamax didn't have that; JVC's VHS standard did.

In summary, you can play a King's Gambit when you have a real network-effect opportunity, racing to market without regard for the costs or sometimes even proper team development. But to have one, you must be sure that you see the following: a true network-based industry in which standards will be set by a democratic process—that is, winning the early primaries will create a self-reinforcing pattern of greater adoption. In addition, you want to ensure that the market can be monetized in a relatively obvious way: sale of product, realization of transaction fees, even advertising. (YouTube didn't have this, but that just proves our earlier point that there are some successful businesses that you can't try to emulate.)

If you play the King's Gambit, good luck. But keep your résumé up-to-date just in case.

The Ruy Lopez

Although far less violent than the gambit openings, the Ruy Lopez is still an up-tempo, pressurizing opening plan that exploits the classic first-mover advantage. Named after the Spanish monk who pioneered it in the 1600s, it is perhaps the most classic of all chess openings. White stakes claim to the sweet spot of the board but, unlike the King's Gambit, doesn't play "irresponsibly" in seeking a quick knockout.

This is what our friends at Email Data Source are playing: well paced but not frantic, spending in line with development, and getting and using feedback to constantly readjust the plan. In the Ruy Lopez, you're always pressing the attack, depending on how the opponent moves; it is aggressive but fluid, not the hell-or-high-water approach of the King's Gambit. The aggression comes in never letting a move go without turning up the heat, matching each move by Black with a different thrust that keeps the initiative. But meantime, we hold onto every pawn.

The business lesson is this: You really can be aggressive and parsimonious at the same time. And given that the Ruy Lopez is the most popular chess opening of all time, you can bet that it's a good recipe for your new venture.

Indeed, there's a deep reason why the approach works so well as a business opening, and it's not the superficial one about simply not liking to lose money. To steer your business correctly amid all the changing business forces today, the only true measure of how you're doing is real market feedback: getting paid.

No matter what anybody inside your organization thinks, no matter how nice the reviews are, no matter how complimentary the analysts may be, one thing is for sure: The highest quality feedback comes from paying customers. Why they are willing—or, as important, not willing—to write checks tells you more than any consultant ever could.

This need to both make product and sell it is another reason why developing the whole team evenly, as the Ruy Lopez requires, is so important. This can be problematic for entrepreneurs, who tend to be great at one of two things: marketing or engineering. Whatever that skill is tends to be wildly overemphasized at the company, while other key aspects of the operation are neglected. A product will often be fully developed before a serious sales group is formed, or sales will promise features that are barely an idea. Customer service functions, financial controls, and simple things like communications infrastructure are ignored. Without all parts of the team in place, the feedback loop on which the first-mover advantage depends cannot function.

So to play the Ruy Lopez, you must develop quickly and evenly. Remember to castle early. But once you've done those things, get a product to market as quickly as possible to begin to generate real market feedback; capture and incorporate that information, and iterate as quickly as possible. Don't waste that first-mover advantage.

OPENINGS FOR BLACK: ATTACKING PREVIOUS MOVERS

The lessons for Black are just as fundamental. "First mover" is no longer the operative phrase, but many of the same rules—develop your team quickly and evenly, generate a feedback loop, and iterate as quickly as possible—still apply.

Rule number one for Black is this: You can't just copy the moves of the other player. If you do, his first-mover advantage should win. You've got to do something different. For example, simply coming to market with the same product that's a bit cheaper is highly unlikely to oust an incumbent: His response may be to simply drop prices until you go away. More is needed.

There are basically two different ways of going about being the second mover. Like the White openings, with one you play to win; with the other, to win gloriously.

The Sicilian

"The Sicilian" has become the most popular opening for Black over the past few decades and is definitely to be recommended to venturists entering an existing market. From move one, it creates

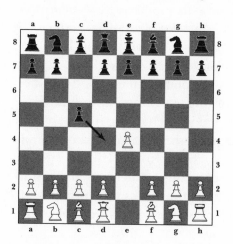

THE SICILIAN: BLACK ATTACKS THE CENTER
FROM A DIFFERENT ANGLE, RATHER THAN
GOING "HEAD TO HEAD".

an imbalance in the position. Instead of going nose-to-nose with the incumbent, *it attacks from a different angle.*

The defining move of the Sicilian is c5 in response to e4. Black is attacking the center, but with a twist. White plays e4, but Black doesn't respond with the classic mirror move, e5. He takes a different perspective on the question of how to win the key central squares and plays c5 instead: an indirect challenge. In the Sicilian, Black often lets White pursue his plans instead of challenging every move with a direct countermove. He sets up his own set of plans based on a different approach. White often launches a Kingside attack, while Black goes after the

Queenside; White's plans often inflict lasting damage on his pawn structure, whereas Black safeguards his in the hopes it will serve him well in the endgame. It's a fight from different points of view.

Playing a Sicilian can help you win against entrenched competition, but you need a new angle, a different approach. Three that often work in the business world are (1) a different business model; (2) aggregation, a differentiation based on bundling other services or products with the product already in the market; and (3) a differentiation based on disaggregating the existing product and targeting a niche market. If, of course, the product is so different from existing ones that you're really going after a new market, then you're playing White, not Black.

So, our three subvariations are listed here:

A Different Revenue Model

Maybe the most famous Sicilian player of all time was King Gillette. But since everyone knows how it rose from obscurity by nearly giving away the razor but charging big for the blades, let's look at the most recent variation on the theme. Surprisingly, perhaps, the newest Sicilian variation is being played by a very old pro.

Kodak is trying to monetize its expertise in imaging by entering the printer market. Well, nothing shocking about that. However, they're reversing the Gillette model: charging for the printer and "giving away" the ink. Their bet is that consumers are tired of being hooked on the drug of expensive ink cartridges and are ready to "kick the habit." They're relying on an unusual assumption about the American consumer: that she's smart enough to make the decision that paying a little more initially will yield lower costs over time.

Whether this ultimately wins or not, it's a very clever attack. It is hard these days to show that one's printer quality is superior to another's; they all seem pretty good. So, how to attack an existing, relatively mature market? From a different pricing angle.

This sort of idea has been successful over and over, literally for centuries. It is, for example, how McCormick tractors got going in the 1840s. The machines were incredibly efficient and undoubtedly a good investment, but farmers simply didn't have the cash to afford them: It required a few crop-years to earn back the high expense of the device. So McCormick started selling on a pay-as-you-go plan and became the dominant industry player. This is also how Xerox finally got people to buy its expensive copiers when carbon paper was so cheap: by charging by the copy, rather than the whole $4,000 price at once. More recently, prepaid phone cards showed that a different charging system, in and of itself, can be a business.

Netflix is another recent example. Although many people would say that its key differentiation is its distribution method, the killer tag line was *no late fees*. Wow! The bane of the video-store customer was not so terribly much driving to the store but, rather, that if you couldn't manage it for a few days, you'd wind up paying more than the original movie rental in penalties (And, God forbid that you dropped the thing behind the couch and forgot about it for a couple of weeks, then you'd have to pay 50 bucks and you'd own it). Moreover, the basic idea that you could watch an unlimited number of movies for a monthly set price was extraordinarily appealing to heavy users. Thus, the pricing model was just as important as the delivery mechanism in the attack.

More recently, turning pricing models upside down is how high-end headhunter sites like Ladders.com and ExecuNet are thriving. Traditionally, headhunters charged the company that hired them a retainer and some percentage of the employee's first year of pay; online job sites have traditionally done the same. Inverting this formula has worked well. The new sites charge job seekers annual subscription fees. Because only "serious," and presumably quality, applicants are willing to pay, the companies get to see a great group for free. That drives corporate usage, which generates more fee-paying applicants.

Search marketing has enabled the most profound pricing twists of all. Today, you really can "monetize eyeballs" in a fashion unavailable to the first generation of Web sites. So, for example, Plentyofish.com has become a tremendous success even though it entered the crowded online dating world late and with a barebones site. But because it doesn't charge users a dime, it caught on, and because the page views can be turned into money through key word advertising, it generates revenues. Indeed, the site is kind of an uber-example of information age opportunities: The whole site and all its infrastructure is run by one guy with the part-time help of his girlfriend. Changing the charging metric to "free" certainly works for consumers, and if you can use modern tools to make the content advertising-supported, God bless you.

Outflank by Aggregation

A second kind of off-center attack has become much more important in the information age, which has made prices transparent and so exaggerated the advantage that buying power and lower prices give large companies. Ace Hardware plays it well, so let's take a look.

How in the world can Ace compete on price with the likes of Lowe's and Home Depot? After all, these behemoths each sell 10 times as much product and enjoy accordingly lower unit costs. Answer: It can't. Similarly, how can Ace hope to offer customers the same sort of amazing inventory the big boxes do? Same answer. But, in four of the past five years, Ace has shown greater same-store sales growth than either of the big boys. What's going on? Ace is attacking the market from a different perspective. Its focus is on convenience and service; these different squares, like c5 for Black, have shown to be incredibly valuable in fighting for the middle of the market.

First, Ace limits its inventory to serve its bread-and-butter retail customers; it ignores many items required by the pros that the big boxes serve. That makes for midsize stores in which it's easy to get in, find what you need, and get out. That also enables Ace to provide better, more knowledgeable customer service in a field where expertise is a critical element. Of course, it's also paying attention to operating efficiencies, as everybody must, but trying to squeeze prices down to directly respond to its bigger competitors isn't realistic. The combination of easy-to-navigate stores and high-quality advice is enough to overcome modestly higher prices. That's an important and easy-to-emulate lesson—which FAO Schwarz is now trying to follow. It may have lost its first game and gone into Chapter 11, but the company is trying for two out of three by switching to the Ace version of the Sicilian.

The venerable retailer forgot its plan when the category killers first showed up in Toyland. It tried to match Toys "R" Us and then Wal-Mart move for move on price, a fool's errand. Far worse, in the effort to do so, it lost its "imbalance," the native advantage discussed in Chapter 6 ("Lucky or Good?"), which was a fantastic, Disney-esque buying experience for grandparents and children. Trying to match the lower prices and enormous inventories that Toys "R" Us offered meant that FAO Schwarz had to cut back drastically on service and store maintenance. So it wound up without a cohesive plan, in the worst possible situation: With neither great prices nor a great place to shop, it was a classic example of no plan being worse than a bad plan (also a "Lucky or Good?" subject). Result: checkmate.

This time, the company is switching to the Ace Sicilian. The goal is to "make it worth $10 more to buy a teddy bear" there through a unique selection, excellent service, helpful advice, and a great experience (not to mention the guy out front dressed like a toy soldier). In other words, it's going to try what it was that made it FAO Schwarz in the first place. Personally, we hate shopping for toys next to discounted laundry detergent, so we wish them luck.

Outflank by Disaggregation

Since the second variation was "beat low prices by aggregating service," it is perhaps not surprising that the third big category is "disaggregating," going to a version of the product with fewer features and a lower price point and aiming it at a specific submarket. The established competitor can't drop prices across the line just to match you in one market.

One of the great examples, although obviously not by a start-up, was Kodak's "FunSaver," the first disposable camera. The big idea was that it was the first camera not intended to replace the consumer's "real" camera; it was just for "oops, I should've brought my camera" moments. (It's a good thing megapixel cell phones weren't out yet.) I remember running out of the Kremlin to buy one in Red Square to record meeting the head of Kremlin security on the day Kasparov introduced us. Whatever you might say about the guy, he had a fine sense of humor: Just as my translator was about to click, he opened his jacket, revealing a tie emblazoned with a giant Statue of Liberty.

Several new cell phones also provide good examples in this day when most are wildly overfeatured. One company is doing well with a version they're marketing to older consumers. It features a simplified keyboard with big buttons but no camera phones or ring tone downloads. Another aims at kids with a phone with just five buttons, one for each number it can call, and a GPS tracker so you can find the tyke if she's late for dinner. (However, in a classic example of missing the real target market on the first try, it turned out that most of these units were surreptitiously packed into the luggage of husbands with suspicious travel schedules.)

"Deconstruction" is not limited to products: It can also work for services. For example, Pangea3 is a "Funsaver" for legal services: an inexpensive, limited-purpose version of your main firm. The big idea is to exploit the fact that India produces its share of fabulously smart lawyers who are willing to work for a fraction of U.S. rates (and that both countries' laws are based on the English system, so the legal training is very similar). Now, these guys may never handle corporate mergers or child custody battles, but they can be ideal for many routine matters, like basic contract preparation, litigation discovery requests, and patent reviews. They don't seek to compete head to head with the traditional law firms; instead, they're targeting the legal services market from a different angle, winning board space.

Alekhine's: Playing for Revolution

So you can see that the Sicilian is a great way to get into the game as the "second mover." The "hypermodern" openings, like Alekhine's, can be, too. But they're not for the faint of heart. They take big risks and seek nothing less than total revolution.

These openings are based on a strange idea: allowing, even inviting, the opponent to establish a dominant central position, and then undermining it with counterattacks from deep in the corners. When first introduced in the '20s and '30s, this heresy against "correct" chess play set off a wild series of games fought with all the ideological passion of the real-world revolutions of the day.

Because business players of these openings seek to fundamentally alter the way large established industries work, they usually fail outright or are very, very successful: Federal Express (FedEx), Dell, and Google are examples. Normally, large amounts of capital are necessary, and because you fundamentally threaten the core model of some big players (rather than just competing on the same basis as they do), they'll go all out to squash you. Playing Alekhine's as Black is a little like playing the King's Gambit as White: either a glorious win or a crushing defeat.

Take FedEx, for example. In the early '70s, there were several large package delivery companies (United Parcel Service, now UPS, DHL, etc.) that controlled gigantic businesses with well-run infrastructures. It was hard to see how they could be vulnerable to attack.

But Frederick W. Smith saw an opportunity to upend the system: Buy a fleet of planes, which no existing company had, and offer an overnight service. At the time, it was far from clear that there would even be demand for such a thing, but that, of course, was the sort of multimillion-dollar gamble that usually comes with playing the Alekhine's.

Certainly, it was rough going at the start; spotty revenues don't match up well with extraordinarily high fixed costs. And some of the target markets were complete washouts: For example, the company had taken its name from the intention to shuttle checks between Federal Reserve banks in order to shorten the time needed to clear them, but the government backed out at the last minute. The story is that Smith got to such desperate straits that he once hawked shares in the company to a local jeweler for watches and paid the staff in timepieces instead of cash.

But eventually the entire U.S. economy opted to accelerate itself by three to five business days. The transformation in the package delivery system was profound, the order completely upended, and the companies that thought they controlled the "center" found that they no longer did. The attacked were forced to become the attackers and still have not caught up.

Dell Computer also targeted an established market in a revolutionary way and made a fortune from it, going from zero to more than $50 billion in revenues in just 20 years. The idea, one could say, was simple: Sell custom-built computers directly by phone (later, the Web) to customers and cut out the middleman.

Selling such complicated devices directly to consumers, without an educated force of salespeople in the middle of the process, was the revolutionary idea. Dell was smart enough to see the rapid evolution of a class of buyers, most of them corporate, that didn't need to see the salespeople in the big boxes.

At a deeper level, his idea took advantage of several truths that others didn't understand, like the importance of customization. Early in the development of the industry, all sorts of hardware options were available that were important to different customer segments (e.g., whether to have a newfangled CD-ROM drive, a graphics card, a bigger memory, etc.). Prices have dropped so far now that it is easy to provide all important features for a modest sum, but back in the day, customization was both important and unavailable through traditional retailers. More fundamentally still, the constant downward pressure on prices makes inventory less valuable every hour: A system that built the units only as ordered made a huge amount of sense.

Armed with these insights and a superb ability to execute, Dell became a supernova. It exploited its first-mover advantage incredibly well and came to understand the nuances of a custom-order business far better than its competitors. The Internet supercharged the entire model because order taking no longer even required phone reps, and customers could learn all they needed to know on the Web. The company utterly upended the industry, shockingly outperforming incumbents like Hewlett Packard (HP), Compaq, and IBM. But as discussed later, they eventually fell victim to the wonderful chess expression, "There's nothing so hard to win as a won game."

Playing the Alekhine's is dangerous: Once a large company has established control over the center of a big market, it has a huge incentive to defend it and to crush disruptive entrants at any cost. But if you have that fundamental business model breakthrough, access to a large pile of capital, and the stomach to play it, the rewards can be breathtaking.

 ## LESSONS

1. The first-mover advantage is real in two circumstances, and the way you play depends on which one you're after:
   a. The network effect: When you have a real shot at a network-effect business, growth is more important than revenues. To win, beat the other players to an industry standard where users both benefit from and contribute to the network. Come home with your shield or on it. Play the King's Gambit.
   b. The classic first mover: Revenues are more important than growth because they provide the highest quality feedback. To win, iterate faster than your opponents. Play the Ruy Lopez.
2. "Second movers" have to attack by doing something different.
   a. Attack from a different angle: a new pricing model, aggregation, and disaggregation are three good approaches. To win, stay away from head-to-head competition until your different angle has captured enough of the market to give you a strong base. Play the Sicilian.
   b. Upend the basic functioning of an established industry by adopting a different infrastructure to deliver the product or service. It's a very high-risk, very high-reward approach.

To win, undermine the broad, established center of a large market with a fundamentally different value proposition. Play an Alekhine's.

3. Forget detailed business plans, but make sure everybody inside knows the "idea behind the business plan."
4. Castle early; establish barriers to entry.
5. Develop the team before attacking; otherwise, you won't be able to exploit your feedback loop advantage.

CHAPTER FOUR

ON THE CLOCK

Run out of time, and you lose. It's the same in business and chess.

Time is the only utterly inelastic resource. There really is no more where that came from, unlike the similar fib told about real estate: There, you can build up or down to increase it. And not only can you not save this precious asset, the opposite is occurring. The information revolution is accelerating time in a very real way.

Mark Hurd, the CEO of HP, has a great expression for it: We're "red-shifting." That's the scientific description of the way that light waves change as heavenly bodies move away from each other at ever-increasing speeds. And, as with a red-shifted planet, the tempo of business change will only continue to increase.

Indeed, the biggest threat many executives face today is not the classic competitor, a company selling the same product. It's the red-shifting business environment itself. Given that, the question becomes, Who sets the agenda? Will it be your more active competitors, or you?

STAY AHEAD ON THE CLOCK

Perhaps the most difficult decision a player has to make is not what move to make. It's how long he can afford to think about what move to make. Indeed, time is often a chess player's worst enemy, more dangerous than the most ingenious opponent.

Wait a minute, you might think, are you kidding? Isn't chess about the slowest game ever, maybe even worse than baseball? Well, forget the stereotypical image of two old geezers staring endlessly at a board in a stuffy club; those guys aren't exactly playing for the world championship. In serious games, there are not one but two kinds of time imperatives.

Let's consider a chess clock. The timepiece is actually two clocks, one for each player. When a player makes a move, he hits the button on top of his clock, which starts the other player's clock running. It runs till that player moves; then that guy hits the button on top of his clock, and it starts the first player's again. In this way, your clock runs only while it's your turn, and your opponent's clock runs only while it's his or hers. Thus, each player's clock measures his own total elapsed time during which it was his turn to move.

In traditional world championship play, the players started with what you might think is a pretty long time to make moves: Each had 120 minutes to make his first 40. But even at this "slow" pace, notice that a player had an average of 3 minutes per move. Time controls in many tournaments these days are much shorter, and some even feature "blitz": just 5 minutes to make *all* the moves in the game. That usually works out to about 7 seconds per move, and there's no safe haven at the 40-move mark; it's sudden death till the end, as the first player to run out of time (or get mated) loses. As the flags are about to fall, the players slam the clock buttons with the staccato of machine-gun fire.

To draw the obvious analogy, Alfred Sloan, the father of modern management, played at nice, slow, classic time controls, but Eric Schmidt and Steve Jobs are speed-chess junkies.

Note that players can allocate their time among individual moves any way they want. That often leads to "time trouble." A player can get lost in thought and spend way too much time on one move, leaving him far too little time for the rest. Players caught on the wrong side of this bind are said to be "behind on the clock." They usually lose. After wasting too much time on finding a "perfect" move, there's so much pressure to move quickly later that mistakes are almost inevitable. That may have an eerie ring to executives caught up in the information age.

The second, more subtle, and equally important kind of chess time is called *tempo*. This reflects the number of moves you have to make to achieve a specified goal. Let's say you open a game by moving out your knight and then use move two to return it to its original square. Now you are back in the starting position, but you've wasted two "tempi." Your opponent (presumably) has spent the moves more constructively. So, if you've each taken, say, one minute to make those first two moves, you're not "behind on the clock," but you are two tempi behind in development, which can quite possibly be fatal against a good opponent. If you're inefficient in using your moves, your opponent will achieve his objective before you do yours, and again, you lose.

BUSINESS TIME

Many companies see the need to regenerate strategy only when their profit margins go south. Why mess with a good thing? If it ain't broke, don't fix it! Well, that might have been fine in the fifties, but in the information age, you're always on the clock. Consider: Where was "the" crisis point for Ford or Polaroid? It's not that they made one big blunder somewhere or that some opponent unleashed a single killer blow; it's that *they slowly got further and further behind on the clock*. The moves just didn't come fast enough.

Of course, these companies saw change coming (we're talking about good management teams) but couldn't figure out exactly how to respond. They froze as their clocks ticked down, thinking ever harder and meeting ever more furiously but not acting. The simple fact is this: If you make moves, you can help shape the future that you're worried about; otherwise, you're just its sitting duck. As Google's Eric Schmidt says, "velocity matters."

The problem, of course, is that this means we have to move before we're sure what to do. But if you wait to move until the perfect answer has been found, here's the guarantee: You won't be the one to find it. Then, while you chase your competitors' approach, they'll have more experience and better customer feedback, so will iterate faster than you. Like Alice, you'll have to run twice as fast just to stay in the same place, and you probably won't ever catch up.

DISCIPLINED URGENCY: FINDING A RHYTHM

It's all about maintaining a rhythm, making small improvements without taking too much time, playing with disciplined urgency. Otherwise, you will lose as surely as a player who just lets his clock run. And like that player, inability to foretell the future is no excuse for inaction.

Apple is doing a lot of things right these days, but one of the most important is the pacing of its moves. Its *rhythm* is setting the agenda just as much as its basic product innovations are.

Every year at the quasi-religious event known as MacWorld, Steve Jobs appears to reveal the great new truths of personal computing. The industry, and even the popular press, is rife with rumors of what this year's revelations will be weeks before the event, and in the few days before the apparition, the buzz becomes deafening.

The interesting point is not simply that "The Blizzard of Ahs" has trained us all to look for his cyclical innovations in what is undoubtedly one of the great public relations circuses of all time; it is that his entire organization is synchronized to these recurring events. His engineering staff, his marketing folks, and his salespeople are all on a rhythm of innovation. They measure their days not with a typical calendar but on Apple's own innovation cycles.

At a deeper level, hitting this pacing means that the company is not introducing products that it expects to be the final iteration. Each is a step further than the last in a continuing progression. Jobs is setting a pace—playing with a tempo—that puts tremendous additional pressure on his opponents.

A beautiful example is the iPhone. Not the cool new features that everyone has been raving about, but something far more subtle and important: It is the first phone to include true auto-updating software. That will provide a permanent "tempo" advantage to the product. Whenever a new feature is ready, it can simply be pushed out to the phones (and whenever a bug is discovered, it can be fixed on phones already in the market), effectively allowing new versions to ship faster, sometimes without as much testing as would otherwise be required.

Indeed, Jobs has been quoted as saying, "If you look at the iPhone, it's software wrapped in wonderful hardware." Pity the other handset companies that have to compete with Apple. On their current business models and technology platforms, they simply will not be able to match the pace of the iPhone's product innovation. (Nor do we think the gPhone will be nearly as revolutionary as people expect: Telephony is complex enough that being able to control both the hardware and the software side—as Apple does—will continue to allow it to move faster.)

On a grander scale, the company is using a quick tempo to gain market share for its computers and, most importantly, operating systems. Jobs recently said, "I'm quite pleased with the pace of new operating systems every 12 to 18 months." Gee, no kidding? Microsoft took seven years to move from Windows XP to DOS, and is not expecting its next system until 2010. The fact that Apple is lapping Microsoft on the development track has everything to do with why its customer satisfaction is so high and why the growth in its computer sales have started running at twice the industry average.

In short, Apple proves the benefit of establishing and using a feedback loop to stay ahead; it has engineered the first-mover advantage into its processes and products. One suspects that this is a lesson learned from two earlier episodes in Apple's chess life.

Believe it or not, Apple's first computer, the Apple I, bombed. But it did not represent a bet-the-company gamble; it was "just a move." That move generated a huge volume of information about what the market really wanted and needed, and as planned, the company quickly made the indicated changes and got the Apple II out to market, which became a huge success.

The second episode demonstrated the opposite and became a model of what not to do. Back when PDAs were going to be the next big thing, Apple tried to revolutionize the market with a product called the Newton (remember?). The company spent something on the order of $350 million to research and develop a radically new product after researching the market in depth, launched a massive marketing campaign to support it, and jammed store shelves full of a version 1.0 product that had plenty of problems. (Its innovative handwriting-recognition software was cool so but flaky and hard to use that it became the subject of a famous Doonesbury cartoon.) But instead of preparing for rapid change and a second version, instead of making a move that was intended to be part of an evolving pattern, Apple had played the equivalent of a big sacrifice that doesn't work. Not that Apple was alone.

Other companies going after the nascent PDA market met the same fate in the same way, including HP, Sharp, and Texas Instruments. Just one was smart enough to play chess with it, to keep iterating the product toward the actual demand that it found: Palm. And that strategy produced a product that made for a successful company for a long time. (Not permanently, of course; no single idea wins a business game any more than it does a chess game, or any more than a single drive or big serve wins at golf or tennis. Indeed, Palm has recently floundered because it failed to keep up its innovation rhythm. It's stringing the good moves and shots together that wins.)

Software development companies illustrate the difference between knowing you're on the clock and thinking you have as much time as you want to move. The choice in software development is to ship on a certain date, dropping any features that aren't ready, or to ship only when it is "feature complete." Companies that do the former and keep their rhythm (like Adobe) are far more successful than those that do the latter. One reason is that the entire company can properly gear itself for the release: marketing, publicity, sales. Another is that engineering staffing levels can be better managed with known dates for product cycles, minimizing downtime and ensuring that adequate resources will be available when necessary. Finally, rarely does the omission of one or two planned features for the sake of shipping the software on time have a profound impact on the product's success or failure. (A note about time-based versus feature-based development processes: When it's time-based, you must be honest about the time. If you give an artificially short period to your engineers, they'll cut out features to ensure they make the deadline. It's OK to overstate goals to sales folks; don't do it with engineers.)

At my old company, the developers created a fantastic system for hitting regular product updates. They were the first to introduce truly modular, Internet-delivered software. Our product was a software version of Lego building blocks: We could change a given feature or add a new one on the fly (say, using video playback) with an auto-update system. Whenever a client machine would connect to the Internet, the desktop software would ping our servers to ask if a new version was available; if so, it would automatically download the new Lego block and perform the swap or addition without rebooting.

The great thing about this was that all our users had the same, and latest, version of our product all the time: All content development work could be done for the new version. By comparison, other software companies had lots of users stuck on, say, version 4 or 5 when version 7 or 8 was being released. By planning and playing a system in which making moves was easy, we stayed ahead of the largest companies in the business for a long time. Eventually, of course, they adopted the same approach, and it has now become standard.

Maybe it's easier to "make moves' as a software company, but that doesn't make rhythm less important for other industries. Just look at Coca-Cola, without argument one of the great brands and companies of the twentieth century and certainly still a hugely successful one, but a player whose opponent has been gaining by moving faster.

Surely Pepsi's rise and Coke's slide can be chalked up to many things, but chief among them was the way the two soft-drink companies reacted to a trend they both recognized in the early nineties: Consumers were beginning to move away from carbonated beverages. Whether for health reasons or just plain changing tastes, the signs were obvious. Pepsi responded with a rapid series of relatively modest moves along a new path, acquiring what would become the leading brands in several categories: bottled water (Aquafina), sports drinks (Gatorade), juice (Tropicana), and through joint ventures, bottled tea (Lipton) and coffee (Starbucks). Meantime, Coke, which actually bought Minute Maid way back in 1960 but never saw fruit juice as an alternative to soda, watched the time drip from its clock.

As a result, Pepsi now controls fully 50 percent of the noncarbonated drink market, which is experiencing double-digit growth while cola consumption falls. As a result of its slow play, Coke has only 23 percent of this part of the board.

Obviously, Coke isn't going to just quit. They bought Glaceau, the maker of "vitamin water," in an effort to fight back, and certainly the game is far from over. But Pepsi's better rhythm has given it the better chances.

Another company with great rhythm, in a completely different industry, is the Icelandic generic-drug maker Actavis. A sign on the door of their CEO, Robert Wessman, sums it up: "The future does not wait." In just a handful of years, his company has grown from revenues of about $60 million to revenues of more than $2 billion, a pace Wessman says is the fastest in the history of the industry. And yet, he does not seem to have taken any irrational gambles to get there.

There is conscious thought behind all this, an affirmative decision to move rapidly and regularly. The CEO recognized some time ago that there are a limited number of significant drugs coming off patent and a goodly number of competitors. The only way to win the upcoming game was to instill a culture fine-tuned to moving quickly but not recklessly.

Thus, he's adopted a rapid but disciplined acquisition strategy, one that emphasizes geographic and product diversity. The trick is to constantly move quickly ("people usually plan things to death") but intelligently (he's passed up several acquisitions that were plausible but deemed too expensive). Moreover, the company spends just as much energy on rapid integration of the acquisitions (especially cross-selling new products in other locations and filling the briefcases of the acquisition's salespeople with existing company products) as it does on the diligence and decision-making process. Actavis is a fine example of playing with a rapid rhythm that keeps the initiative and has the opponents back on their heels.

American Capital Strategies (ACS) has a similar story. It makes many quick, small moves inside an overall plan. Instead of searching for the headline-grabbing megadeals that most private equity firms covet (and require because of the massive assets under management), ACS is a "business development company," which allows it to raise money from the public quickly on an as-needed basis and in relatively small doses. This funding mechanism is a beautiful thing: ACS can pursue its niche (small buyouts) without assuming too much capital on the one hand and without deal-by-deal lengthy and uncertain pitches to institutional investors or lenders on the other.

Like Actavis, the key point is that the infrastructure is built for speed and intelligent risk taking. It has 150 or so deal finders spread out around the country, whose suggestions are fed into groups of operational talent for rapid review. The whole process funnels into a weekly investment committee meeting. And their due-diligence-and-documentation troops form a "SWAT team," ready to execute any approved deal quickly.

Even large consumer staples companies can play with rhythm. For example, 3M has long mandated that 30 percent of its revenues comes from new products each year. That is a huge number for a large company, and only by establishing a deeply ingrained expectation of regular change can it be reached.

What you can't do is delay moving just because you're not certain how to play a new trend.

Major new technology and globalization trends can present big problems but often are not themselves as overwhelming as the paralysis created while they're analyzed. Your clock is ticking! Make a move in line with the trend, see what happens, and move again. To see the two different approaches at work in the same industry, compare Verizon and the old AT&T.

As we write, the single biggest threat to the telephone business is voice-over Internet protocol, or VOIP. It obviously challenges

Verizon's traditional landline business, but less obviously, it also threatens the cell phone business of Verizon Wireless, its 55 percent-owned subsidiary. After all, as the ability to wirelessly connect to broadband networks increases, so will the ability to replace cell phones with VOIP calls. Many companies, faced with such a broad and frightening trend, would ratchet up marketing for the old services and defend their turf like Davy Crockett at the Alamo . . . with approximately the same result.

Despite the massive uncertainty it faced, Verizon did not wait around, hoping the VOIP situation would clarify so it could find the "right" move. Instead, like a matador sprinting after the bull rather than just avoiding it, Verizon is rolling out a new VOIP service of its own, along with new fiber-optic cable lines. As a result, even though the traditional landline business is indeed suffering (how could it not be?), subscriber sign-up for its fiber and VOIP services have been tremendous, portending a bright future for the company.

On the flip side, let's take a look at that great business behemoth of the twentieth century, AT&T. Oh, that's right, we can't: That company doesn't exist anymore. It's a corporate King Lear whose kingdom and name were rudely taken by its greedy children (while another of its offspring, Lucent, née Bell Labs, suffered a forced marriage to a surly French prince, Alactel—ouch).

What happened? Fundamentally, AT&T simply couldn't figure out what to do when the Internet revolution began to transfer the economic value of communications away from its proprietary network. Instead of aggressively pursuing new avenues, using its vast technology and people assets to try different moves, it spent its time protecting its franchise, much, as it turns out, like a child protects her snowman on a warm day.

A similar tale can be told about the *Wall Street Journal.* Like Coke and AT&T, there is no doubt about the heritage of its owner, Dow Jones, or its commitment to excellence. But the controlling Bancroft family was simply too slow to respond to market changes. The moves they thought about while the clock ticked down, but didn't make, included purchasing 50 percent of Comcast in the 1980s, creating options tied to the Dow, and the purchase of Financial News Network (the current CNBC, throwing off hundreds of millions per year). Their slow play allowed lesser-known companies like Bloomberg and Thomson to become the leaders in financial information. Then, behind on the clock, they made a classic time pressure blunder: With heavy pressure to just do something, they bought Telerate for $1.6 billion, only to mismanage it and sell it off years later for $500 million. (The CNBC purchase, in contrast, would have cost $90 million.) Slow play had its inevitable result: The family had to give up its seat at the chess table in favor of Rupert Murdoch, who plays blitz with the best of them. It's now his game.

One last tale of woe features perhaps the most underappreciated product development company in U.S. history, Xerox. Here are a few minor things it developed: the mouse, the graphical user interface (GUI), the system for networking computers, and e-mail. So why do we still know it as "the copier company"?

You guessed it: Xerox simply moved too slowly. Oddly, Xerox did in fact produce the first computer to integrate a mouse and a GUI, in 1973. But the next move came eight years later, a pace that would cause a forfeit in even the slowest chess time controls.

Meantime, in 1980 Steve Jobs took a tour of Xerox Parc in a visit paid for with a substantial amount of Apple pre-IPO stock. He instantly saw what Xerox did not, and Apple immediately began development of the Lisa.

Xerox finally moved again in 1981 with the Xerox Star. It was the first commercial system to incorporate various technologies that today have become commonplace in personal computers, including a bit-mapped display, a window-based GUI, mouse, Ethernet networking, file servers, PostScript, and e-mail. But Xerox overpriced it, did not market it well, and again failed to iterate toward a market. Soon thereafter, Apple introduced the Lisa, which also flopped because of a still-too-high $10,000 price. The difference, however, was what the two companies did with the lesson. Apple accepted the market feedback, moved again with a much lower-priced Macintosh, and introduced it with the famous 1984 Super Bowl commercial. Just as the commercial promised, the future of computing was forever changed—and it didn't include Xerox.

There's one more, almost poignant, worthy point about Xerox's slow play. It finally thought to sue Apple over the appropriation of these magnificent inventions; but the time quite literally had run out. The three-year statute of limitations had expired, and the suit was dismissed.

Early in this game, Xerox was far ahead in material, resources, distribution, and just about every other relevant aspect. But it lost. The difference was simple: Xerox played at a classical time control; Apple played speed chess.

LEAVING YOUR FINGER ON IT

I'm sure you've seen beginners play. They'll take a piece that they want to move, push it to the intended square, and then leave their forefinger on it while they look around for what they might be missing. This goes on a while, and then the piece is withdrawn to its original square. Fortunately, real chess has a "touch-move" rule: If you touch a piece, you *must* move it somewhere. Leaving your finger on it is illegal. It should be in business, too. For even more appalling than companies who get frozen in their tracks by a new trend are the ones who really do see what's coming, prepare a response, and then fail to pull the trigger.

In a chapter about clocks, a perfect example is the entire Swiss watch industry, or what's left of it. When semiconductors became widely and cheaply available, it was pretty clear to everybody that they could be used to make inexpensive, accurate watches. The Swiss, being the bright lads that they are, fully understood that their precious mechanical movements would be no match for the accuracy and low cost of the new entrants. So soon thereafter, they did develop a low-cost quartz-powered digital watch.

Then they kept their finger on this move while their clock, so to speak, ticked away. It was just too painful to give up on the tradition, the classic marketing message, and the time-honored production methods. They decided to try a compromise that would let them keep selling their expensive mechanical models as they slowly introduced the cheaper, semiconductor-based products to the market.

But as always, there were many others who also understood the power of the new technology and would not wait. The Hattori Company in Japan, which had also been making watches for years, saw the same move but played it immediately. As the Swiss tried a slow switch in a futile attempt to preserve the old, more profitable luxury end of the watch business, Seiko watches became the dominant global brand.

THERE'S ONLY ONE PRIORITY ZERO

Another variation of the problem arises when executives make decisions but fail to take the steps necessary to implement them. In classic chess, when a player decides on a move, he writes it down on a score sheet, rather like a golfer keeps a record of his game. He then reaches out, makes the move, and punches the clock. In business, some moves don't get made because even though decisions are made and recorded, no one reaches out to change the organization. As in chess, just writing it down doesn't make it happen.

Look at how Siebel Systems "decided" to add a professional services component to its model of selling customer relations management software. The CEO said they would, the press releases said they would, and the analysts said they would—but the organization simply didn't respond. Writing it down didn't make it happen: The salespeople wouldn't change their focus from the higher-commission software sales to the lower-commission service deals. (That is a particularly common problem in implementing major shifts. As one exec I know says, salespeople are "coin operated"; big-picture corporate strategy is not their thing.) Largely as a result of its inability to effectuate its stated decision, the company had to sell to Oracle, unable to compete even with an upstart, Salesforce.com, in the industry it essentially invented.

In a similar way, Kodak, for example, failed to execute on its initial decision to go digital in the late nineties. The decision was made, but the old-line executives simply kept doing what they had been doing. No one was responsible for actually implementing the change, and inertia prevailed. Now, CEO Antonio Perez says, "you have to burn the boats," quoting the Conquistador Hernán Cortés. Only 3 of the 21 senior executives who were there in 2003 are still there today, but there's no doubt now about its new focus.

These sorts of problems arise simply because everyone at the company keeps operating in the old way. Surely, they think, what they have always done remains important, so they just keep doing it. This is where you should remember the favorite rule of Anders Vinberg, my old CTO and now a distinguished engineer at Microsoft: There's only one Priority Zero.

In chess, you obviously can make only one move at a time. There may be an overall plan with many facets, but there's just one, single, next move. Execution occurs. Companies at turning points must act in the same way, making the change the company's *only* goal: If other priorities are not abandoned, old behavior is easy to justify. A few key executives must be made accountable for implementation; the decision isn't really made until somebody moves the piece.

The Priority Zero rule is not just useful when attempting to institute a major change; it should be writ large at the top of every off-site whiteboard for it is often the very act of creating lists of priorities that keeps them from being accomplished. After the lists are drawn, people tend to effectively dedicate themselves to one task (often the one they suggested—and why not, it's on the priority list!), others to different ones. Everyone will feel good, working away on priority issues, but none will get done.

THE PLAYER DECIDES

Yet another key reason that companies fall behind on the clock is the mistaken belief that the management team must reach consensus before acting. Needless to say, getting different perspectives on a situation and generating a solid two or three "candidate moves" (see Chapter 4) are exceptionally important ideas. That said, however, a decision to do one (and to create a single priority zero) is the executive's responsibility.

Fortunately, a player doesn't have to cajole his Knights and Bishops into agreement on whether to attack that weak pawn on d5, but many executives feel the need to achieve harmony among their staffs by having everyone agree to every plan, even though—very naturally—they all have different agendas to push and internal organizations to protect.

This is like getting a unanimous verdict from a jury where some of the members are related to the plaintiff and some to the defendant. The only way to consistently get agreement is to consistently compromise. The best-case result is a watered-down version of the best idea; at worst, a strategic Frankenstein is born. That's not management; it's abdication.

Playing Too Fast

One of the best reasons to put your company on the clock is this: When the (inevitable) unexpected events occur, they don't create panic in the organization. The company is used to responding to events with a new cycle of innovation. Like a baseball team that knows it'll get its own turn at bat soon, a company whose culture is based on the clock does not overreact when the opponent scores some runs. Faced with adverse developments, it has an infrastructure and culture that permits intelligent, considered, and relatively rapid response.

By contrast, moving too fast in response to an opponent's move almost always results in unnecessary mistakes, disrupting the organization prematurely, and failing to fully capitalize on opportunities.

Perhaps the best example of this syndrome was the company that should have dominated the interactive ad-serving world, DoubleClick. Clearly, it was "in the right place at the right time," having gone public in the late nineties with what became the industry standard ad-serving system. They were also the first to control an ad network and the first to sell search listings. In other words, they had, back in 2000, the package of strategic building blocks that Google and Microsoft have recently spent fortunes trying to assemble. All that and a six-year head start! What in the world went wrong?

When the tech bubble burst and its revenues temporarily dipped, DoubleClick began to panic, making too many moves too quickly in an effort to shore up revenues. It bought all sorts of companies that were vaguely in the Internet marketing space but without any apparent overall plan. Aside from poor integration and execution, some caused tremendous problems, like Abacus, an information-gathering company, the acquisition of which led to the first great Internet privacy debate.

But ill-considered acquisitions were not its worst moves. Early on, DoubleClick had been one of the first companies to knit together a network of sites to which it could serve its ads and then act as a selling agent for those sites. This network business was an ideal complement to the ad-serving technology it could also provide (and, of course, the two sides of the business could work together beautifully). But when the Internet ad market temporarily went south after the tech bubble burst, the company naturally saw revenues on the network side shrink.

It reacted like a chess beginner spooked by an unexpected move and sold it off, one of the most colossal business misjudgments of the Internet age. Within 18 months of the sale of its hard-won business, ad networks became the rage. Who really cared about relatively generic ad-serving technology? The key was to own the sites to which the ads could be served. (This is what propelled Yahoo!'s recovery from the tech implosion: It was itself an ad network.) Similarly, DoubleClick gave up way too soon on its efforts to sell search listings for Alta Vista; had it stayed in that game, it would certainly have been in a position to buy Overture (as Yahoo! did) or even Google.

In short, the company had an overwhelming strategic position in the greatest growth industry of the past century and blundered it away by moving too quickly. Its remaining assemblage of technology cats and dogs remained an unintegrated mess for as long as the capital markets would allow. It was swallowed by a private equity company in 2004, spiffed up a bit, and then sold to Google in 2007, providing a supremely ironic bookend to the story.

THE EXECUTIVE'S CLOCK

I have an amusing proposition for you. Go out and buy a chess clock for your desk. Two days later, you'll be shocked by what it shows.

Milbank, Tweed is one of the handful of great global law firms, and time there ingrains many lessons about success: It demands excellence, zealously nurtures relationships, and balances tradition with creativity. The surprise was that it also taught me almost as much about time management as it did law.

As you know, lawyers charge by the hour of work performed. So every law firm has a billing system that requires attorneys to record time spent, usually down to the quarter hour. At the big firms these days, associates are routinely expected to bill in excess of 2,000 hours per year, or about 40 hours per week for 50 weeks.

Doesn't sound all that onerous, you say? A kinda normal work-week, right? Well, just try it. Seriously. Get out a sheet of paper, keep it on your desk, and record all the time you spend actually working one day.

Let's make two bets: First, over the course of an averagely difficult day, you will not "bill" more than 5 hours. That is, when you remove all the aimless chatter, trips for coffee, reading of newspapers, IM chatting, walking the halls, Net cruising, lunchtime, and personal calls, you would only bill 5 hours in good conscience on even the most demanding day. Note that this 3-hour discrepancy adds up to 15 hours in a normal 5-day workweek, and at that rate you'll wind up with 1,250 billable hours in your first year, which will, therefore, also be your last.

Bet number two: You'll forget to record your time quite often. And when trying to reconstruct what happened, you'll then overstate the time actually worked both because one, you don't really remember, and two, there's a lot of pressure to win our first bet (just as associates face a lot of pressure to meet their billing goals). You won't lie, exactly; you'll just misremember in a convenient way.

For proof, on day 2, use the chess clock. It's weirdly easy to get in the habit of punching the button every time you stop or start a real work task; the other clock will be recording the time you're wasting. It will record the competition between productive and unproductive time exactly. Compare these results with those you recorded by hand for the first day. If it's more or less the same sort of day, you'll see that I win.

Now think how bad the problem is for an entire company, an entity composed of individuals who each fall prey to this kind of blindness and for which, as to the collective whole, no one is even trying to record time. Yikes!

A CHESS TRAGEDY

Confession: I killed a Grandmaster with a chess clock once, right in the plush offices of Milbank, and it wasn't just any GM.

Of all the great chess players that have been, perhaps the most beloved is Mikhail Tal, the "Magician of Riga." The nickname came from his slashing, daring, amazing attacks that appeared out of the clear blue, and his appeal to average chess players was something like Arnold Palmer's was to the golfing public. Although he held the world championship title for only a brief time, he was one of the handful of strongest players in the world for most of his life. Toward the end of his career, he was known as especially fearsome at "blitz," the five-minute-per-player version of the game, in which the combination of his ferocious attacks and not enough time for his opponents to find the right defense made him the world champ even late in his life.

Tal was a good friend of my chess teacher, Grandmaster Roman Dzindzichasvili (pronounced "Gingy-hash-veely" and always shortened to "Gingy"), a regular at the Wall Street Chess Club. Gingy himself was one of the top ten blitz players in the world, and so when we heard that Tal would be in the city, we arranged an exhibition match. It drew the biggest crowd in the club's history, even attracting New York TV reporters, a true rarity for chess.

Tal and Gingy got there early and were hanging out in my office, along with several other GMs. They amused themselves by playing warm-up blitz games with each other—where the ebb and flow of the games were far too fast for a guy like me to hope to follow—when someone came up with the brilliant idea that Tal should play his host. The ever-gracious Tal turned to me, smiled, and waved toward the chair that Gingy duly vacated.

Well, I've been pretty nervous a few times in my life, like during my stumbling first presentation to a jury. But nothing compared with that moment. I often think it must have been like what the writer George Plimpton felt when he lined up as quarterback of the Detroit Lions. Of course, there was absolutely no chance of winning; it was simply a question of how badly I'd embarrass myself in front of all my GM friends, my teacher, and my law partners. Could I possibly manage to lose with a shred of dignity? Against the Magician of Riga, probably not.

But what could I do? Stoically, I grinned, nodded, and made it over to the table. As is the etiquette, he took a Black pawn and a White one off the board and put one in each hand behind his back, then brought them out in his closed fists. I picked one, and he opened the hand to show I'd chosen Black. Great, I thought, might as well start off at a disadvantage, too. Oh, well, it hardly mattered. We did the customary handshake over the top of the board— really, a big honor in itself, like teeing off with Tiger Woods—and we began.

Tal's first few moves were standard: a Ruy Lopez. OK, good, at least he wasn't going to try to blow me off the board with some wacky opening. Or so I thought until move 5, when Tal played something that I had never seen before in my life. He was apparently offering me a pawn "for free," but even though I couldn't see what was coming, I knew perfectly well what this meant: the start of the kind of vicious attack for which Tal was famous.

I froze. My nightmare was about to come true: absolute humiliation in a few moves. I was far too panicked to actually analyze the situation—as if, with Tal on the other side, that would've mattered, anyway. All I could hear was my clock ticking loudly. I looked up and saw every GM in the room staring at me.

There is an old saying in chess: The best way to refute a gambit is to accept it. So even though I had no idea what the right move really was, I figured I'd take the pawn and at least go down like a man. Looking up, I saw my teacher smile; I wasn't sure whether it was of the paternalistic or sadistic variety.

Tal instantly replied, and I was on the clock again. Damn, now what? My fear level hadn't declined, and I really couldn't even try to understand an already complex board situation. My knight was under attack, though, so I just moved it to the first legal square I saw. Very, very fortunately, this turned out to be "book," so my position didn't totally collapse instantly. Tal moved again, and so did I—and again. I was still alive, although in a terrible bind. He kept squeezing and squeezing, like a boa constrictor slowly eliminating every possible movement by its victim. He was taking squares away from me on every move; all my pieces were jammed into the corner of the board. It felt like Dunkirk without the rescue boats.

I almost literally had no legal moves left and was about to resign when . . . Tal reached out to shake hands, signaling a draw! At first I was just a touch angry. To offer a draw at this point was like letting your four-year-old tie you in a footrace. Sure, you're killing me, but there's no need to be condescending on top of it.

But then, seeing the turmoil in my face, he pointed at the clock. I hadn't dared even look at it during the game. Both flags were down! If only one is, that guy loses. But if both fall before anyone calls it, it's a draw. The several Russian GMs present were utterly stunned, crushing me in embrace, shouting wildly; one produced a bottle of vodka. I even got the only hug of my career from Gingy. Tal, always the gentleman, shook my hand but was also shaking his head, undoubtedly thinking his age was finally starting to take a toll. A mistake like that, even playing "client chess," was absolutely bizarre for him.

I've never felt such a burst of relief and exhilaration. An actual draw versus Tal! OK, he wasn't really trying all that hard, but still! It was the talk of the club all night long.

I wish the story ended there, but it doesn't. One of my friends had taken some pictures, and a few weeks later we had them developed. I was gleefully reliving the highlight of my chess life, thumbing through the photos, when one in particular caught my eye. I stared at it, squinting at a key detail. What I saw was utterly deflating.

We had barely started, but the flags were almost down. Nobody had reset the clocks after Tal's previous game with Gingy, so he had started the game with only a minute or so, not five. I didn't draw him. It was all a terrible mistake.

But the worst part of it might be that I never saw him again to tell him. The poor man died soon thereafter, an event certainly hastened by his dismay about drawing a patzer like me.

 ## LESSONS

1. The most successful companies are built to deliver rhythmic change.
2. Don't try to build the perfect product in version 1.0; it's not going to happen, anyway, so get something out there, take the feedback, and iterate. Then do it again.
3. You can't avoid moving because you fear damage to your existing business model: If you don't do that damage, the market will do far worse.
4. Unexecuted decisions haven't really been made; a serious move must be "priority zero."
5. Moving too fast and without a consistent plan is just as bad as moving too slowly. You must give ideas time to ripen. Rhythmic change helps avoid this problem just as much as it does moving too slowly.

CHAPTER FIVE

BAD
BISHOPS

Can working with the six kinds of wooden pieces that comprise a chess team really tell us anything about managing people effectively?

Yes, it can. In chess, unlike the other big strategy games (go, checkers), each side comprises pieces with different abilities and values to the organization. And, as in any company, the most basic abilities are held by the greatest number of participants (the pawns, each side has eight, and the commonly ascribed numerical value of each is 1) whereas the greatest ability, and value, is held by the fewest number of participants, the Queen (each side has just one, and its value is 10). In the middle, we have a few players with moderate abilities, the manager-level Knights (3 points), director-level Bishops (3.5 points), and VP Rooks (5 points each).

The really telling point concerns the "big dog" himself, the King, which has almost no power at all but, because his loss is the end of the game, is considered of infinite value (judging by the size of the now common exit package, about the same as current CEOs).

The art of management is, of course, getting people with different skill sets to collaborate to achieve the overall corporate objective. For this, a few hundred years of chess play have provided some powerful lessons.

Chess players refer to their more potent players as "pieces": the Rooks, Knights, Bishops, Queen, and King. Strategies to maximize the power of this executive team are the subject of the first half of this chapter. The second half concerns the pawns, a group much under-appreciated by average players and executives. But Grandmasters know very well how the misuse of a single pawn can doom the enter-prise, and their methods are ever more relevant to modern com-panies as the information revolution continuously pins more of the corporation's fate on its nonexecutive knowledge workers.

Now, HR types might argue that this whole analogy is unfair: After all, chess pieces move only in certain ways, while humans have many more "degrees of freedom." To which I say, show me an executive over 30 who's ever really changed his or her stripes. Sure, in principle they can, but sadly, life is too much like chess in this regard. My experience is that people are who they are. Just like chess pieces, they really only move in certain ways, regardless of how many seminars you send them to.

Biz devs seek to solve every problem through a new deal, the CFO's plan is always to cut costs, salespeople vault over every issue with loftier revenue projections, and engineers always think tech-nology is the answer. People who are recalcitrant and fear risk-taking, who are more comfortable pointing out the downside than taking a chance on new opportunities, will always be so. Folks who only see rainbows, always will. It's all very well to talk about train-ing and personal growth, but, in the end, just like chess pieces, a given person is limited to a given set of responses to any situation. Indeed, even the identity of the employer and the job description are nearly irrelevant. People will see problems and opportunities and then attack them in the same way they always have.

That's why the Peter Principle resonates so loudly: At some point in the promotion cycle, you're asking people to change behavior.

My partner Jim Peet tells a relevant story from his days at McKenzie, the famous consulting firm. He was helping a software company analyze some product issues. In reviewing the sales pipeline reports, he came across a particularly large potential trans-action that was listed as having 50 percent probability of closing that quarter.

When he interviewed the salesman about it, Jim asked why he'd handicapped it at 50:50. Answered the sales guy, "Well, there's an established vendor that we're trying to replace."

"Oh, I see. So, what, you have a particularly good relationship there?"

"Uh, no. I just met them recently. And they really like the guys they're working with."

"So, we're offering a better price?"

"Not really. We're actually a little more expensive than what they're using."

"That's not good. What, then? We have new features they need?"

"Can't say that. We're missing one or two things they're looking for."

"Well, if there's an entrenched competitor with a better product at a lower price, I don't think I'd list it as a 50 percent probability. Why did you?"

"Because I'm in sales."

Indeed.

THE EXECUTIVE TEAM

There is a simple but profound rule that will immediately improve the results for any novice chess player and all executives: Get your pieces to the right squares.

What does that mean? It's pretty straightforward. It is your job to put the pieces in position so that they have the *maximum scope.* What good is a Rook if it's trapped in the corner behind a wall of pawns? Very little. In fact, in the opening parts of the game, one of the main objectives is to get that Rook over to an open file so it can exercise its power. Similarly, if you put a Knight on the edge of the board, you've got a big problem: The number of squares it controls is down to four from a potential eight. (The chess expression for this is, "Knight on the rim, prospects are dim"—lame, but accurate.) Nobody wants a job where you use only half your talents. That guy is going to be looking for a new player to work for soon!

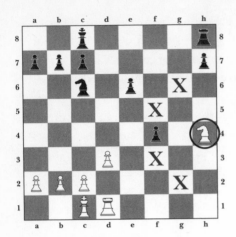

HOT JOBS KNIGHT
(THE XS SHOW THE SQUARES
THE KNIGHT CONTROLS)

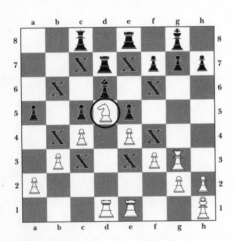

KNIGHT WILLING TO WORK WEEKENDS
(THE XS SHOW THE SQUARES
THE KNIGHT CONTROLS)

Buried talent is not just frustrating for the employee, it robs the organization of its power. Which raises this important question, Which "piece" should be used for which job?

BISHOPS AND KNIGHTS

The "which piece" problem is especially critical in organizations attempting to launch a new product or strategy. The characteristics that make people successful in managing a mature organization, and thus make their owners more visible to senior management, are fundamentally different from those necessary for success in an entrepreneurial environment. The safe choice is thought to be the person with an uninterrupted chain of successes on his or her résumé, but the better choice is likely to be the less-well-known employee who's had experience with those kinds of problems, with making these sorts of moves.

Maybe that "Bishop" has indeed had an uninterrupted series of successes in managing different divisions of the company. But those jobs were probably actually similar: They always required a straight-ahead operational discipline with few unexpected obstacles.

Great for a Bishop, which only moves in straight lines. But when the job requires the ability to make sudden 90-degree turns and hop over unexpected obstacles, you need a Knight. Maybe that employee only made one or two previous moves in the game, not enough to have earned the trust of management. But skills are far more important to success than levels of seniority: No matter how much success that Bishop has had for you lately, it's not a Knight.

We see this issue over and over again at the New York Angels, our venture investment group. Start-ups frequently hire proven executives from a related industry in a search for experience and credibility for their enterprise. Such decisions are almost always disasters for both the company and the executive. The 20-year industry veterans are rarely prepared to change their points of view rapidly and execute the sudden shifts crucial to any new venture. They struggle without large support organizations that can make their directives happen and budgets they consider inadequate. They're Bishops, not Knights.

So whether you're involved in developing a new venture for a large company or are launching a start-up, choose the right piece: the less-experienced one whose skills are better suited to the task over the person who's proved wildly successful at a fundamentally different job.

Bishop Pairs: 1 + 1 = 3

When the game starts, each side has two Bishops. Given the way the pieces get set up, one of these starts the game on a white square and one on a dark square. Now, Bishops are powerful pieces: They can move any number of squares along any diagonal. So, if you put one in the dead center of the board, it controls a whopping 14 squares. Note, however, that because diagonals are formed by squares of the same color, the Bishop that begins the game on a light square will always stay on light squares, and the dark-squared Bishop is similarly fated.

Meanwhile, an individual Bishop is considered only slightly more valuable than an individual Knight (3.5 points to 3). It's a bit odd, then, that a player who retains both his Bishops into the middle

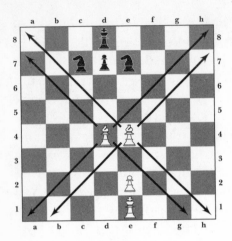

THE BISHOP PAIR

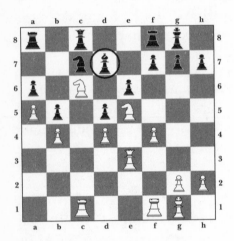

BAD BISHOP: GREAT PIECE, NO FUTURE

game is thought to have a huge advantage over an opponent who does not. Why should two Bishops be considered so much better than two Knights? Because, when the Bishops cooperate, no square lies beyond their control, and they can control huge swaths of the board, like machine guns set up shoulder to shoulder.

One by itself cannot get to half the territory on the board, but the Bishop pair is an awesome weapon. They are the classic $1 + 1 = 3$.

OK, so it may sound like something from one of those insipid "inspirational" wall posters in an employees' lounge, but the point still begs to be made: The two Bishops are an obvious lesson for executive teams. Sales managers and CFOs travel on opposite-colored squares; so do general counsels and biz devs, and the CTO and COO usually do, too—marvelously skilled all, but typically limited. Pair them up, however, and you cover all the squares.

A large technology company we know uses this idea to perfection. When faced with some stubborn issue, the CEO assembles a small executive team to tackle the problem. No matter the nature of the issue, it's always addressed by two executives—always an "opposite pair." "When we work this way, the issue gets looked at from very different perspectives; there's often a clash, and a quality solution is far more likely to emerge," the CEO says.

BAD BISHOPS

Now let's talk about the flip side: What to do about an underperformer?

We just learned that, in general, Bishops are a bit more valuable than Knights and that two Bishops operating together are really scary. But sometimes a top player will intentionally trade a Bishop he has for the opponent's Knight. Why would he voluntarily do that? Because the Bishop is "bad." Take a look at this diagram.

It so happens that all of White's pawns are sitting on white squares, so White's Bishop has nowhere to go; it has no real future prospects. It doesn't matter that the Bishop *would* be a great piece if those pawns weren't there. As this board sits, the Bishop is inferior to that Black Knight, which can hop around over the locked-up pawn structure.

This piece, sad to say, is not pulling its weight. Now, we have to agree that it's not the Bishop's "fault": If the pawns hadn't been put in its way, it'd be a great piece indeed. And, after all, the Bishop has been with us since the start of the game, so we'd hate to let it go. But any good player, or CEO, would exchange the Bishop for that Knight in a heartbeat.

We see this situation in companies every day. Many are full of "bad Bishops": great folks with good talents but in positions where those talents aren't able to move the company forward. Because the people are good and skilled, the situation isn't really their fault, and we feel loyal to those who've been around a while. So they stay. And stay. And stay. But it's nearly always detrimental to an organization for a host of reasons. And it's bad for the employee as well; if she were in a game without all those blockading pawns, her career might be skyrocketing.

The problem arises frequently in maturing companies where formerly desirable entrepreneurial behavior becomes trapped by the need for process. It is also common in companies that have shifted their business model or sales pitch. One company I know recently added services as a key element of its previous software-only sale and wound up firing its previously best salesman as a result. Explaining the benefits of technology consulting was very different from showing standard power points about prepackaged software. The company suddenly had a bad Bishop on its hands and had to swap him out.

Of course, you hate to fire anybody, but no GM lets affection get in the way of an effective organization, and you can't, either. If it helps, you can take your inspiration from one executive I know. Faced with the unpleasant executioner's duty, he had a ritual. Right before the termination interview began, he would hold up his hand in the "Mr. Spock" fashion, palm up and facing away from him, with the fingers splayed two each side. He would then recite the Vulcan creed: "The needs of the many outweigh the needs of the few." Then the victim would be led inside.

And if you need a little more incentive, think about the observation of Sarah Fay, the CEO of Carat, USA. After the fact, have you ever decided that a firing was a business blunder? She hasn't, and doesn't know an executive who has (nor do I). Conversely, every boss remembers keeping bad Bishops around too long, and creating, as they do on the chessboard, lasting structural damage.

DON'T GET OVERLOADED

As every competent person knows, there's a massive downside to that trait: All the work flows to you. Up to a point, that's fine, but eventually it becomes detrimental to the organization.

The problem is most acute in smaller companies. It's well known that few entrepreneurs wind up running the mature companies they started, and the main reason is their inability to delegate effectively. Why are they so bad at it? Because entrepreneurs don't need to be told what to do and cannot understand that others do. Founders simply know what's required, they do it, and they expect others to have the same mind-set. Almost every one of them will tell you, "If the office bathroom needs to be cleaned, I'll do it." Yes, that's great, and it's the kind of spirit investors like. But in a real company, that actually needs to be someone else's job.

It's a common problem in chess as well, known as an "overloaded piece." You love to see one of these in your opponent's camp. For example, a Queen might be doing too much by defending several of her pieces at the same time. This almost always creates an exploitable opportunity for the opponent. The trick is to force her to come to the defense of one of her pieces, and then to pick off the pieces she's left unguarded.

A particularly potent illustration involves a rapidly growing manufacturer we know. They have typically sold their machines for cash, but it's much more profitable long term to lease them out. Shifting business models, however, would require a big new loan facility for buying parts. And given some of the previous debt covenants and the complexities of the particular industry, arranging and closing a deal like that is a ton of work.

What's the problem? An overload. It turns out that the CFO is also the best relationship and salesperson in the company, and every time he makes progress on getting the new loan deal in place, he has to hit the road to save the quarter. Then the financial figures change, and the analysis and negotiations have to start over. He's an incredibly potent piece, but darting back and forth covering too many objectives is killing the company's longer-term profitability.

Avoiding an overload means attacking the root of problems and delegating, rather than just doing the undone things yourself. If slow sales are a problem, find out why. Don't just hit the road yourself to close deals. "I'll do it myself" is the first reaction of any true entrepreneur, but as in chess, it leaves the organization vulnerable.

Becoming an overloaded executive by doing other people's jobs screws up their own sense of what their job is, makes them think there's not much point in even attempting to do it themselves, and worse, has a similar impact on all the other folks who see it happen (and they will). It actually becomes an excuse for poor performance, not a remedy for it.

An overloaded executive is building an organization that is "one genius with a thousand helpers." Any success will be temporary.

PREVENT PINS

Frequently a critical moment comes when a Bishop or Knight, generally of modest value, gets "pinned" or put in a situation where it cannot move because doing so would result in, say, the Queen being captured.

Pins are devastating. In the corporate world, they often arise as the star-employee syndrome. Because an employee delivers, we give her the resources to do more and hence make her more valuable. The cycle keeps going until she effectively controls large parts of the company's revenue stream or development process. Even though these kinds of folks frequently don't show up on the org chart, they become disproportionately critical to the company's success.

This syndrome is dangerous for a simple reason: The organization cannot permit them to move. It is exposing itself to a pin. The employee can make almost any demand, from compensation to product development, and it will have to be met. Like a Knight caught against its King, the employee has developed a value far out of proportion to the rest of the organization.

I've seen this happen many times. A particularly painful case involved my own start-up company and its superstar engineer. He was a charismatic hypergenius who came to dominate the company's culture. At the time, that seemed fine. After all, his team's code was the horse we were riding, so why argue? But then we realized we were pinned.

His personal ideas about product direction took precedence over needs the sales staff identified, but we couldn't move him out. He began having views on every aspect of the company's operations, causing midmanagers fits, but we couldn't effectively control him. Finally, a large potential corporate acquirer realized that they could simply hire him away for a fraction of what it would cost to buy the company and then just build a system similar to ours. When our guy explained what the offered pay package was, all we could say was "Congratulations." So he wound up moving anyway, and we nearly lost the game as a result.

The only reason we didn't was because the then-No. 2 guy refused to go along. Thank God! He was also an utterly remarkable talent who had quietly been living in the superstar's shadow for years. He understood everything about the code, had brilliant ideas on where to take it, and his hard-working style quickly won over the previous superstar's cult. Indeed, the company performed even better thereafter, without the dysfunctions that superstars can cause, intentional or not.

Admittedly by accident, we had done what chess players do to break a pin, interposing a piece. That is, we had inserted another piece immediately behind the superstar. When you fear a pin, immediately insert a No. 2 and force the spread of knowledge, contacts, and methods. One star employee simply cannot be allowed to keep sole control of all the key knowledge and people along with her incredible talents. Get into a position so that, if you do lose that piece, it will hurt, but the damage can be withstood.

So, to summarize our executive team HR rules:

1. Put your pieces on the right squares: Make sure to put them in places that take advantage of their strengths (Knights in the middle, Bishops and Rooks on open files and diagonals).
2. Pair team members with their opposites so that the things one cannot do, the other can; use Bishop pairs aggressively.
3. Immediately trade off "bad pieces," no matter how much you like them.
4. Do not allow overloaded executives (including yourself) to cover for others' weak performance.
5. Prevent pins by interposing people behind your superstar employees.

THE KNOWLEDGE WORKERS

"Pawns are the soul of chess," wrote the great French player Philador, just as his countrymen made a similar but broader point down the *rue* at the Bastille. (By the way, he was also perhaps the

first player to routinely astound audiences by playing games blind-
folded, a feat that terribly worried his friends. Denis Diderot, for
one, constantly urged him to abandon such performances to preserve his sanity.)

Peter Drucker, the father of modern management theory,
must have been channeling Philador, when, in 1954, he wrote,
"Employees are the essence of the modern corporation." Until
Drucker, most management experts thought of employees as an
expensive necessary evil in the production process, and the whole
idea of managing them was to minimize the related expense and
trouble. The proposition that they were actually powerful assets
was a breakthrough. But I'm not sure even Drucker foresaw just
how critical lower-level employees would become in the information economy.

Today's "knowledge workers," as Drucker liked to call them,
are with increasing frequency the real store of a company's value.
They are a different breed from their forebears for one main reason: Their decisions and actions can affect a company's success as
profoundly as any executive behavior. Today's "pawns" might be
deciding which chemical formula to pursue, how to implement
that new feature the marketing department has demanded, how
to get to the logo the new clients want, which materials can handle how much stress in the engineering design, or how to interpret
those scrawls in a patient's chart.

And unlike employees of the past, today's workers can and do
move in a heartbeat to a better opportunity. (By the way, one interesting side effect of this trend is the decreasing frequency of hos-
tile takeovers: "The assets go home at five" and won't come back
the next day if they don't like the new management.

Today's employees' motivations are different, too. The ground
troops of the information age are as interested in job satisfaction
(*nothing* is as frustrating to a software developer as absolutely great
code that sits idly on a few hard drives in the lab, instead of being
out there on users' machines), a flexible schedule, and the quality
of their working relationships as much as they are in a straight pay-
check (ah, for the good old days!).

All in all, then, management of the company's knowledge workers has become one of the most critical and difficult jobs an executive faces. Yet, it is a subject that is often ignored as the senior team focuses on "more important" issues like product development schedules and sales pipelines.

Similarly, pawns are ignored by beginners, but they are of the most profound importance at top-level chess. Pros fret over pawns that become "isolated" or "backwards"; conversely, "connected" passed pawns (those that can no longer be blocked by the opponent's pawns) are usually a winning advantage. But any pawn, if supported from behind so you can push it, can reach the ultimate rank and get "promoted" into a Queen to provide the next generation of leadership on the board.

This almost eerie echo between chess and HR terms is no accident. In the care and feeding of pawns lie powerful models for managing the people whose daily activities are determining your company's success or failure. If you look at a chess board in the starting position, you can see that the big pieces are completely hemmed in; they have nowhere to go. Unless the pawns get out front and make some space for them to operate, the executive pieces will be sitting around at "HQ," doing nothing the whole game. (Yes, yes, many pawns would say that happens no matter how well they do their job, but that's for later.)

Turning pawns loose to perform at their highest levels will make all the difference in your game. There are three basic rules for maximizing pawn power: Use pawn storms, ensure diversity, and lead from behind.

PAWN STORMS

The idea of a pawn storm is simple enough: A few pawns line up and charge down the board in lockstep, protecting each other as they go.

They can chew up big chunks of board real estate and, once they get rolling, be as merciless as a rising tide. You see it coming, but there isn't much you can do about it.

And that's the model for getting the most from your knowledge workers. Small bands of closely knit, relatively independent software developers, designers, researchers, product managers, engineers, or account reps can deliver huge wins for a company. If you properly establish these teams and send them "down the board" more or less on their own, you'll have a far more potent organization.

The positive dynamics of a small group of knowledge workers can be an awesome thing to see. A small group working on a discreet problem can operate more efficiently and with instant-feedback loops that drive ideas far faster than can occur in larger groups. They easily distribute information internally; develop their own internal languages for their goals, obstacles, shortcuts, and strategies; and create realistic schedules. The excitement of real progress that this tends to bring drives far more productivity than do deadlines imposed by "Corporate." They do not need and do not want daily instructions from their boss on how to spend their time.

The gang approach is great for customer and account teams, engineers working on specific development efforts (many people say the first known successes of small teams occurred at NASA), designers, even groups tasked with developing new internal processes. For example, over a single weekend, we had a group of four engineers solve a core problem with a graphics display that had bedeviled AOL for years. Gangs are particularly effective in crisis mode when speed is most critical and the stress involved can break down the dynamics of larger groups.

Adobe uses pawn storms to great effect in a formal program. It encourages small groups of engineers to develop ideas in a process run by the Corporate Development Group. The trick is that, after a while, the seed idea has to find sponsorship from a senior executive who helps clear away internal process constraints. In this way, Adobe can test cool ideas without overinvesting in them too early.

One resulting product is an online tool that lets users of social network sites edit their videos for posting. Conceived by a small, independent team focused on opportunities for video in the consumer space, the company launched the service much faster than it could have through standard product-planning cycles. And it's not just a useful service. The funny thing is, because of the way it's used, those sites have become resellers for Adobe. Thus, the storm unleashed both a new product and a novel business model.

This doesn't mean these teams require no management at all. You do have to buy them pizzas. In fact, this actually has an important benefit, noted by Amazon's Jeff Bezos: If you can't feed the whole team with a large pizza, it's too big. Somewhere around five or six seems to be the magic number. The hundreds of new-product teams at 3M, for example, average about that.

The idea doesn't just work at technology companies. Empowered teams of "pawns" are crucial to the success of PrintingForLess.com, one of today's fastest-growing young companies. PFL provides high-quality printing services for small and midsized businesses. It's based in Livingston, Montana (population 6,851), and has grown from a start-up in the mid-nineties to a large and profitable enterprise today. But how do they distinguish themselves in what most people consider a "commodity" business in this day and age?

Pawn power. A customer's interactions with the company are through a three-person team, a group of folks who create the trust you need to commit an important, relatively big-budget project to some "cowhands" you've never met. They do a great job of demystifying the world of high-end printing to first-time users (what is CMYK, anyway?) and escort customers through every single step of the process with lavish personal attention. I had the "Eagle" team on my project. One of them is always around, and that person always knows exactly what's up with your project. Almost as important, the team members are empowered to cut deals with you (oops, maybe you're not supposed to know that), so that a wavering customer is nailed before hanging up the phone in the first call. Team pride is apparent when working with these folks; you almost get to the point where you'd feel bad saying you weren't happy with the finished product (in fact, we always have been). And after you're done, there's lots of follow-up, staying in touch and looking for that next job, which you'll likely give them.

Largely as a result of this pawn-powered approach, the company now claims more than 40,000 customers and has been recognized as one of the fastest-growing small companies in America.

DIVERSITY

A more subtle but crucial point that chess teaches us about a workforce is that diversity is truly essential. Now, is this just some stupid point made for the sake of political correctness? Not from me. It is a smart point made for the sake of success.

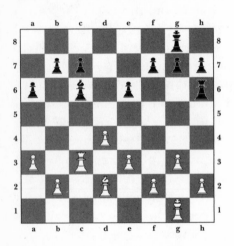

A FATAL LACK OF DIVERSITY

If you're playing the White side, how do you feel about your pawn structure in the diagram? Beginners probably think it's fine, but at a glance, advanced players would be terrified to play it. Why? Because White has a permanent weakness on the light squares around the King. All those pawns are sitting on the same-colored spaces, which means that because of the ways pawns have to capture, they are also defending solely squares of that same color (here, dark ones). The position has huge holes defined by the light squares, and an attack on those squares will probably prove fatal.

Organizations composed of people who are too much alike are always vulnerable to competitors that come at things from a different angle and always blind to market trends emanating from outside their common culture. Baseball teams need right- and left-handed batters so as to not be overly vulnerable to a given pitcher; football teams need to run and pass to keep defense from focusing on one or the other; basketball teams need short guys who can bring the ball up and distribute it, not just seven-foot monsters in the middle.

Businesses need people of all stripes to deal with the outside world successfully. Without diversity, like a chess side with a "color weakness," they are vulnerable. It's not just that the culture struggles to market to diverse customer sets or to work effectively with partners and suppliers of different backgrounds. Just like the side with a color weakness, the organization is blind to trends and products coming at it from a different angle. And like that player, you can't fix such problems quickly. Diversity must be part of the game plan from the beginning.

"Mentoring" a Passed Pawn

OK, so we know that connected passed pawns are almost unstoppable. But how else do we get big things out of our nonexecutive personnel? Well, you probably know that a pawn, if pushed all the way across the board to the last rank, can be turned into a Queen. Fantastic, but not so easy to pull off. The trick in chess—and, it turns out, also in business—is to lead from behind.

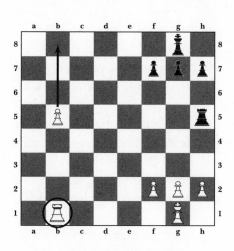

LEADING FROM BEHIND:
THE PERFECT MENTOR

Good players know that you always want to support a passed pawn from the rear, not from in front, as the Rook is doing in this picture. It stays rooted to b1, protecting the pawn on each forward step: b5, b6, b7, and the glory square, b8, on which it is crowned as a "new executive."

This is also the right style with humans because although everyone praises mentoring, not all mentoring is the same. A mentor who is out front in meetings, or with clients, often comes off as the Sun King, graciously allowing some of his reflected glory to fall on his protégé. It's condescending and, whatever everyone may say, hardly inspires the confidence of peers, executives, customers, or the protégé himself. Conversely, quietly sitting behind the scenes but pushing, encouraging, and counseling is far more likely to provide the genuine personal growth everyone wants to see.

Bruce Chizen, the CEO of Adobe, knows how to be that supporting "Rook," just like he knows how to unleash pawn storms. One of his engineers was passionate about developing a next-generation eBook reader that would essentially be a "media player for books," combining text and video in a lightweight software client. Few at the company believed in the guy, but Chizen did. He stayed deep in the background but encouraged and pushed the guy forward, meeting with him often and providing the cover of his name when necessary. It was the engineer's project, not Chizen's, all the way through. After two years in the making, it was formally launched in 2007, a plus for the company and a big step down the board for the engineer.

PROBLEM PAWNS

Compare the earlier happy story of a pawn storm with the woeful tale of "doubled isolated pawns," where one of your pawns is standing directly in front of another, and they have no pawns next to them on either side.

Unlike pawns in a phalanx, these jokers can't defend each other at all. Like two swimmers in shark-infested waters, they can only helplessly watch as the other gets picked off. A "backward" pawn, whose buddies have charged ahead down the board, has similar problems: Because it can't be protected by its peers, it's likely to fall.

Like bad Bishops, it is usually best to swap out weak pawns ASAP. But these days, even the most meritorious firings can lead to lawsuits if the groundwork isn't properly laid. Many executives don't bother because they're sure the underperformer already knows how he's doing (after all, the executive does!). Wrong.

People hear what they want to hear. Nearly everybody thinks they're doing their job well or if not, that it's the fault of other folks in the organization. I've seen scores of exit interviews in which employees reported that they'd never been told about their shortcomings and are shocked when the axe falls. Where exactly, they demand, was the problem?

Chess players often want to know the same thing after they've lost a game. They think they played OK but somehow failed. That's why all serious players write down every single move as it's played. Even years later, they can go back and point out exactly where the problems were. Executives need to be in precisely that position for underperforming employees.

Preparing reviews is boring and slow and delivering them unpleasant. It's easy to let them slide, but you can't. As Sarah Fay says, "Every day I get up, look in the mirror and yell at myself: 'Reviews are *not* a waste of time!'" It may startle your spouse, but it's good advice.

Everybody has a story about their most difficult "fire," but my own concerned a fantastic guy who worked for me as a lawyer early on. He was extremely pleasant to have around the office but just took forever to get things done. We anguished over what to do, but eventually decided that we had to let him go.

On hearing the news, he paused, slowly looked up, and finally said, "But I don't really think you can do that. You're discriminating against me."

"Holy cow!" I thought in a brief moment of politically correct panic, "We can't do that!" But then, after a moment of reflection, I realized I couldn't think of a single atypical characteristic he had. I was staring at a perfectly normal-looking, well-formed 30-something white married man. I squinted, looking him up and down for a clue. Finally, sensing my confusion, he said, "Because of my disability."

Huh? He was a star on the office softball team, didn't stutter, and so, after a few more minutes of running through my mental catalogue of possible handicaps, I could only look at him and say, "I'm terribly sorry . . . but what is it?"

"Well," he said earnestly, "for several years now, my brain has tended to see what it thinks I want to see, rather than what is actually on the page. It really makes it difficult to understand or draft contracts."

"Uh, so you're saying we can't fire a lawyer who can't read and write?" (We did.)

LESSONS

1. Believe in pawn power. Knowledge workers are just as valuable for an organization as any executive. They demand and deserve respect and opportunities to contribute.
2. Create gangs to attack specific problems and let them go.
3. It is essential to create a team whose members are not alike. Diversity is defense, not liberal pandering. Ask Mother Nature.
4. Lead pawns from behind.
5. Repeat after me: "Reviews are *not* a waste of time!"

Chapter Six

Lucky or Good?

Here's an interesting exercise: Do some research on the topic "business and luck." You will find almost nothing. Apparently every successful business was well planned; every failure, explicable.

A bit fishy, eh? Indeed. Think back again about Yahoo!. One rather doubts that Jerry and David foresaw how aggregating their favorite URLs would become a $40 billion business. So, then, were these guys just lucky? Let's hold onto that thought for just one minute.

When great players sit down at a board, they know what opening they're going to play if they're White, and depending on White's first move, they know what defense they'll play as Black. So plans exist, and then the game starts. When it does, there are no bad bounces or poor calls by the ref. Weather is rarely a factor, and few games have been lost by reason of a devastating midcontest injury.

Nonetheless, with all the planning, limited options, and apparent absence of luck, the games invariably veer off into unforeseen territory almost immediately. Think about the brilliant checkmates that have dazzled fans for centuries: were they foreseen when the game began? If not, were these outcomes just lucky?

Johnson Controls presents another curious case. Founded in 1885 by Warren Johnson, inventor of the electric room thermostat, it has been cranking away in pretty much that same business ever since, sometimes buying related ventures like York, the heating and air conditioning company. Oh, yes, it also purchased a car battery company in the early part of the century and then started producing "control"-type auto parts, like electronics, lighted mirrors, and car seats. But they've certainly stayed true to their "Big Idea" the whole time.

Now, after more than 125 years of thematic moves, they've gotten what looks like a big break. The green movement has suddenly jerked energy efficiency to the top of everyone's list, igniting demand for products the company claims can cut the costs of heating and cooling in new construction by 50 percent or more (like CO_2 detectors that monitor how much exterior air is entering the building and thus allow for more exact temperature control). Similarly, the company's battery business has become a top performer as cars go electric.

So the question, as it was for Yahoo! and Morphy, is, Did Johnson foresee all this? Was the 1920 Globe-Union Battery Company acquisition aimed at dominating the 2010 market for energy-efficient cars? Did the CEO of 1960 identify a 50-year plan contemplating that global warming would bring the company riches? Presumably not. So were they, too, lucky?

Perhaps it's a matter of semantics. Clearly, the fact that Yahoo!, Morphy, and Johnson Controls were following a plan was critical to their ultimate success, and yet, just as certainly, unforeseeable events occurred once or many times to push them over the top. Ditto with basically every other success story I can think of.

All of them involved an element of, well, maybe "randomness" is a more neutral word. And why not? Physics proves that uncertainty is a fundamental part of all phenomena, baked as deeply into nature as sugar is in a cake. It would certainly be surprising if business activities did not share this characteristic.

Why, then, does our search for "business and luck" turn up so few results? How come serious researchers and the popular press don't focus a bit more on this subject? One assumes that it's fear that randomness undercuts their basic value proposition: You can't teach or explain luck, after all.

Or can you?

It boils down to what that great business thinker, Branch Rickey, used to say: "Luck is the residue of design." So it is. Sure, Yahoo! and Johnson Controls got lucky to some extent. But if they hadn't been doing what they were doing, following a plan and working hard, nothing at all would have happened to them. If you have a decent plan and keep plugging away, making the best moves you can in trying to improve your position, good opportunities are far more likely to arise than if you play randomly. The expression, "the harder I work, the luckier I get," is not just cute; it is mathematically accurate.

Contrary to the apparent fear of business pundits, then, there's no harm admitting that great success involves luck. The harm is in acting as if no luck is involved (as the successful usually believe) or that only luck is involved (as the lazy protest).

All of which means that design is not definitive, but it is crucial. To maximize your chances of success, you do have to have a plan, and you do have to bang away at it.

The Nature of Plans

Yahoo!, Johnson Controls, and Morphy followed a plan. But each plan was general, and the battles and minibattles that arose were certainly not preordained. Their plans were not highly detailed, move-by-move blueprints—that would have been impossible—but, rather, a general direction to which the companies and players stayed true as the contests raged.

This brings us to a wonderful and highly prevalent confusion of language. In response to the direction that "clear" plans be devised for the following year, the vast majority of business-planning exercises generate reams of detailed projections and forecasts, most of which become irreversibly wrong within a couple of months. The confusion is this: *Clear* does not mean "specific"; it means "clear."

While it is indeed true that we must understand what we're trying to accomplish, that does not mean we can accurately predict specific developments, the order of the steps, or even what the steps will be. Moves must be made on the basis of the real-time position, not on what we expected it would be when we thought up the plan. They must be independent but cannot be piecemeal.

And the plans must be dynamic, subject to change as the feedback loop—the opponent's and market's responses—is evaluated. As James Brian Quinn, the father of Logical Incrementalism, says, "The validity of the overall strategy lies not in whether it is maintained intact, but in its capacity to adapt successfully to unknowable realities, reshape itself, and ultimately use resources most effectively towards selected goals."[1] Or more simply, as Peter Drucker wrote of the planning process: "Objectives are not fate; they are directions. They are not commands; they are commitments. They do not determine the future; they are means to mobilize the resources and energies of the business for the making of the future."[2]

In later chapters, we'll look at the most important kinds of plans chess players use. For now, the essential point is to understand what a plan in chess is and is not. It is not a deep prognostication of the future position. Instead, it is *a thread of thematically linked battles,* with the goal of creating an exploitable difference in the position. These battles are, like the links of a chain, necessarily related to the previous ones and the ones that follow, but they also have independent existence.

Yahoo! and Johnson Controls followed this sort of path, but another recent example is Akamai. Like the others, it had a great Big Idea, and the implementation has been a series of struggles, each of which changed the underlying plan somewhat. But Akamai also demonstrates another critical factor in both business and chess: the power of tenacity.

Akamai's Big Idea, born in the late nineties, was a new answer to the question of where the "brains" of a large network should reside: in the network infrastructure or in its nodes?

The Internet disrupted the AT&T network because, as computing power and bandwidth became free, a stupid network with smart terminals (the Internet and its nodes, computers) became far more efficient at data delivery than a smart network with stupid terminals (the AT&T dedicated switching network and its stupid nodes, telephones). But the best possible answer, thought Akamai, was somewhere in between. Yes, a completely stupid network might be better than one with all the answers built in. But maybe a network capable of pulling some report card "C's," and that could also work with the smart terminals, would create maximum efficiency.

So Akamai began placing its own network servers all around the world, essentially creating a shadow Internet, with two major purposes. First, the system could analyze Internet data flows and, like a helicopter reporter, steer packed traffic around jams. For really popular content, the system could replicate the data being requested and store it on multiple servers around the world. With "multiple originals" spread around the globe, no one server would be overwhelmed.

This was a really, really expensive idea. No problem: IPOs were easy in those heady days. The offering was incredibly successful, too successful, really, because the wildly rabid reaction of the markets was actually signaling an impending crisis. And, indeed, a few months later, the Internet bubble burst.

For Akamai, this was a multifaceted disaster. Aside from initiating a stock price implosion that reduced its market cap by 99 percent, the collapse tanked most of the company's customers (including, very nearly, my own company). Suddenly Akamai had neither the market cap to sustain the tremendous operating losses its plan envisioned nor the customers to buy its services.

Even worse, the company's founder, Daniel Lewin, was then killed on 9/11 while on United Flight 93. While single-handedly fighting four hijackers, including Mohamed Atta, he was apparently stabbed from behind by a fifth he had not seen.[3]

But Akamai stuck with the Big Idea, even though it had to make desperate changes in its plans and management to stay afloat. The cuts were mind-blowing: Operating expenses went from $2.6 billion in 2001 to $327 million in 2002. Of course, that meant enormous changes in the rollout plans, and they *still* lost $182 million that year. Meantime, the stock continued to get pummeled as people still wondered what you'd do with all that bandwidth (just like they had wondered what a Xerox machine could be good for so long as carbon paper was cheap).

Again, they had to change the direction of battle somewhat. The refined sales pitch became, Pay us to prepopulate our distributed server network with your content and thus assure fast access to your Web pages. Then, as the online world began to reawaken in 2003, a major cultural crisis occurred that clearly demonstrated the profound need for more intelligent bandwidth: The Web-only broadcast of the Victoria's Secret Runway Show crashed. That event marked the real beginning of superintensive multimedia deployment and, in combination with the explosion in overall Web usage, ended the questions about how you'd ever use all that bandwidth.

Ever since, the company's revenues have been on a steady march upward and have more than doubled over the past couple years. Their model has been proved, and the stock has increased in value more than 100 times. The budding TV-over-the-Web trend and the rapid adoption of VOIP for phone calls, underscore just how prescient Akamai's Big Idea was all along.

Needless to say, none of this was contemplated in the multiyear business plans that accompanied the IPO. Akamai's ability to stick to a Big Idea in the face of so many gut-wrenching developments is a fine example for any company.

By contrast, executives who make planning into a madly elaborate process full of long-term financial models and then dictate that Wall Street cannot be disappointed and that the projections must be met at any cost, are simply mocking the fates. And the fates deliver revenge, as any Dell, Enron, Computer Associates, or Worldcom executive can tell you. Conversely, companies that learn to both stick to a core idea *and* constantly adjust it, like Yahoo!, Johnson Controls, and Akamai, have a shot at the Grandmaster title.

EMERGENT OR DIRECTED? POSITIONAL OR TACTICAL?

Given that plans must exist but also change, how are such changes determined? From an academic point of view, we're at the crossroads of the "directed" versus "emergent" strategy discussion here.

As we know, the problem with fixed, long-term, directed strategies is that—annoyingly—reality always intrudes. Even if a company does not encounter the dramatic obstacles faced by an Akamai, a few weeks after the planning session, you'll get an e-mail about a competitor launching a product that you've just started to design. Or maybe it's the flip side: Someone in the company has come up with a breakthrough that deserves evaluation long before the next planned internal cycle. These are emergent developments that we have to react to, and we need a system that allows for such changes without throwing the whole plan in the blender.

Players face a similar set of problems. There's a master plan, but all of a sudden the opponent decides not to cooperate or, conversely, to over-cooperate and create a big opportunity we hadn't expected. The way a player responds, the way he integrates emergent and directed strategy, is reflected in the interplay between positional and tactical chess play.

Earlier in the book, we talked about ideas like "putting your pieces on the right squares," "opening files" for your Rooks, and exchanging "bad Bishops." These sorts of moves are sometimes called *positional*. They are clearly positive but do not have the decisive delivery of checkmate as their explicit aim. They are "natural." The pieces want to do the right thing, to go to their best squares, to avoid creating big holes in the position. They follow what is for them commonsense rules. They "know" what to do most of the time. During these periods of play, the strategy is emergent: It is being carried along by the everyday actions of the players.

But sometimes a clear path to winning major material, or even checkmating the opponent's King, will emerge: Indeed, the whole point of playing positionally is that, when the level of favorable imbalance gets high enough, a specific set of tactics will generate a winning advantage in the game. The pieces cannot see this grand plan; simply getting on the right square or avoiding doubled pawns will not create a brilliant checkmate. For that, a directed strategy is needed.

So mostly, choosing positionally strong moves that are consistent with the overall plan is the way to go. But sometimes forcing lines appear that can create a winning advantage, and when they do, they must be pounced on without distraction or delay.

It's the same with businesses. Most of the time, things chug along with small moves generated by the organization's normal processes as particular departments or individual employees find new ways of doing things, identify new market segments, develop logical product improvements. The company is naturally following an emergent strategy as the Big Idea progresses. This positional play is best in most cases.

But occasionally a winning tactical line does emerge from the positional improvements. The really great managers see these and seize them and then drive all of the organization's efforts to win the piece or get the checkmate. At this point, emergent processes have to take a back seat to a strong, directed strategy.

A famous example was Intel's shift out of DRAM chips and into microprocessors. Although considered one of the master-stroke moves in industry history, it was actually initiated by positional moves from the middle managers. Those managers had decided to rank the priority of wafer starts by the projected profitability of the resulting product. Initially, the limited-purpose microprocessors made little money for the company and therefore were at the tail end of the priority list. But as competitors came into the DRAM market and prices fell, microprocessors became relatively more profitable, a trend reinforced by their improving utility. This self-adjusting mechanism eventually pushed microprocessor production to the fore at Intel; after a while, it was the only place the company was really making money on its chips. Presented with this breakthrough observation, senior management got the message and enforced a directed strategy: It made the emotionally difficult but absolutely correct decision to exit the DRAM business altogether. The company began to pour all of its (large) research-and-development budget, all of its marketing dollars, and the entire infrastructure of the company into microprocessors. Management saw that the classic Bishop sacrifice was the way to go. An emergent strategy created by midlevel management became a strong directed strategy, and by playing the sacrifice, Intel emerged as one of the great companies of the century.

A similar process led to a crucial breakthrough for Wal-Mart. It established its second store in a small town near its base in Bentonville, Arkansas, for simple logistical convenience. This was a positional move, chosen as employees simply did their jobs, thinking about the easiest ways to move inventory around. But suddenly senior management saw a crucial idea: That second town was just barely big enough to support a Wal-Mart and thus too small to also support a competitive large discounter. By selecting its sites properly, it could effectively preempt competition.

This basic point became a core idea for Wal-Mart's expansion strategy: It could effectively lock up one local market after another by moving into cities of a certain size. The pieces and pawns, in filling their normal functions, made a choice to do things a certain way. But the senior management had to see the real beauty of this approach and then command that it should be a model for all future expansions. So the strategy process went from emergent to directed, from positional to tactical.

This constant interplay between positional and tactical play is an ideal for companies to shoot for: Moves will mostly be positional and emergent, but occasionally that line of play will create a great tactical idea that must be seized and implemented by senior management in a directed strategy initiative.

The Planning Process

OK, so we know that we have to have a plan, that it has to be very flexible, and even that the plan will sometimes emerge from our normal positional play and sometimes be directed at major turning points. That said, if we're sitting down to make plans, exactly how do we do it?

Chess players generally follow a path that has been described slightly differently by various authors but which can be synthesized like this: First, analyze the current position to find your key advantage; second, imagine how exploiting that advantage could lead to a "dream position"; third, work backward from the dream position to find some move patterns that will get you there; fourth, analyze those couple of patterns more deeply to choose one; and finally, of course, adjust as you go along to take account of the opponent's moves.

We'll examine this process in more detail later, but it's first worth noting that while the Grandmaster approach is different from traditional corporate procedures, it somewhat resembles "discovery-driven planning," one of the more modern theories of corporate strategy development.[4]

Discovery-driven planning (DDP) begins by imagining a new product and specifying what its minimum financial characteristics would need to be to consider it a success: something that would constitute a dream position. (This is almost the opposite of the normal corporate planning step one, which starts by taking existing markets and trying to project their future sizes in an effort to determine which to attack.) DDP then examines what assumptions must become true to reach that position—or, in chess, what order of moves would be necessary to get there. Third, DDP mandates making small moves in the direction of the goal but in a careful, testing way in which feedback is closely examined to ensure that the plan is on track, just like the chess analogue.

Both Grandmaster and discovery-driven planning begin with a desired future position and then works backward. In contrast, with the more traditional approach, current trends are projected forward and then plans are made to target the largest projected markets. In our hyperdynamic information age economy, that's a much riskier approach.

The reason that chess beginners are so bad is this: They are asking themselves the wrong questions. That's why most strategic planning processes miss the mark, too.

Novices ask themselves questions like, "Can I take the other guy's Queen?" or "Can I check his King?" Of course, neither is aimed at the kind of Big Idea necessary to create a lasting advantage; these players are asking themselves the wrong questions and therefore are going to make a bad move.

Back in the day, I used to conduct new-lawyer orientation programs at my firm. About the middle of the first day, I'd ask these newbies what they'd do if a client called up and asked them a specific legal question. Maybe the call went, "Is there a special license requirement for owning a dry cleaning operation in New York?"

Eager beavers all, they would suggest running to the library, asking a more senior associate, or writing a memo on the question for the partner to review. All of which were wrong.

Why? Because it's a dead cert that the client asked the wrong question. After all, if the client could actually spot the legal issues in its deals, he sure didn't need a fancy law firm to help. Anybody can look up rules.

The right answer was, Ask the client why he's asking. In this case, he was considering the purchase of a chain of dry cleaning establishments; the price looked good given the profits the chain was showing. Fine. But what the client didn't know and the young lawyer probably wouldn't find with such a narrow question in his head was that the state had recently passed some new environmental laws that would require significant new investment by dry cleaning operators over the next few years. So much for those expected profits. No wonder the chain was for sale.

I had a professor at Florida State who would drive us nuts making this point. For an entire semester, he would answer every question from a student, every single time, with, "What's the answer? What's the question?" It still echoes in my head.

It's one that more corporate planners should ask themselves. Instead, the traditional planning session begins with "How much bigger will the market for X be in three years than it is today?" and the answer is generated by extrapolating from current trends. That creates two problems. The first is that the answers are inevitably wrong. As Bruce Chizen of Adobe says, "I always look at those numbers and always ignore them." He's got history on his side: Just go back and examine as many Gartner and Forrester multiyear projections about future market sizes as you like. These highly respected firms have all the data, well-trained analysts, and access to all the executives they can possibly interview about where markets are headed. They work hard, they think, they carefully crunch the numbers, they discuss, and they then issue reports that are not only never right but often so wrong that they make General Custer's estimate of the attacking force look reliable.

But the deeper problem is that, like chess beginners and my green lawyers, these sorts of planners are asking the wrong question. Even if they do spit out accurate numbers, financial analysis will never be able to account for strategic positioning. Chess proves this point beyond doubt.

As you know, even supercomputers cannot foresee all the possibilities of a chess game. They can evaluate all the options, at the most, tens of moves ahead. But then what? They still have to decide how good the resulting possible positions are, keep a table of those evaluations, and then play a move that leads to what they "think" is the best one. Pretend that the positions shown in the diagram here arises at the end of, say, a 15-move-deep analysis by our friendly computer.

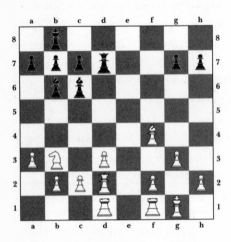

THE PROBLEM WITH NUMBER CRUNCHING

Now, the normal way to evaluate a chess position is to total up the point count on both sides. As discussed earlier, in point-count systems, pawns are worth one, Bishops three, and so forth. OK, look at this diagram, in which it's Black turn to move. Under the standard point count system, White is way ahead: He has two more Rooks and a couple of extra pawns, a whopping twelve-point advantage. So should a computer playing White make the move that leads to this position? Nope: Black can play his Queen to h3 this move, and White then has no defense to the coming checkmate, when Black pushes his Queen to g2 on his following turn. (Note that the White pawn on f2 is pinned by the Black Bishop on b6, so it can't get out of the way for his own Queen to help out.) The material situation tells only a small part of the story. *That's exactly why straight financial analysis is such a limited way of making business judgments.*[5]

Companies that make all their decisions on the rational basis of typical financial planning tools are like rudimentary chess computers, making superbly detailed projections but, in the end, failing because they do not properly account for the strategic situation that exists at the end of the calculation.

The Secret: Identify the Imbalances . . .

So how do we go about making plans? The wonderful chess instructor, Jeremy Silman, explains the Grandmaster planning process in his book *How to Reassess Your Chess*.[6] He starts with a quote from the *Encyclopedia of Chess*: "Planning is the process by which a player utilizes the advantages and minimizes the drawbacks of his position." Now, perhaps this seems like just more consultant babble; it sure sounds like something I heard once while nodding off in a seminar.

But he goes on to his critical point: "You have to be aware of the magic word—IMBALANCE. An imbalance in chess denotes any difference in the two respective positions. *The real goal of a chess game is to create an imbalance and try to build a situation in which it is favorable to you*" [emphasis added].[7] So, first you identify your imbalances, and then you devise a plan to expand and exploit them.

In chess, examples of competitive advantages, of imbalances, are things like a lead in development, superior minor pieces, a spatial advantage, a material advantage, having the initiative, and a better pawn structure or a passed pawn. In business, the most important analogous factors are a leading product, better core technology, better R&D capabilities, a strong brand, cost and manufacturing advantages, a superior distribution system, control of suppliers, a talent advantage, a location advantage, superior financial resources and infrastructure, a more nimble organization, better customer relationships and communication, and intellectual property rights.

And we must examine the other player's advantages just as thoroughly as our own. This is not just in order to play better defense, but because in predicting responses to your moves, you must expect the opponent to make the best move that is consistent with his own plan, and this is not necessarily the move that will maximally interfere with yours.

If you recall, we discussed this point up front in Chapter 3, "First Mover." It's the answer to the question, "why couldn't Google do this, too?" It *could,* but you must *expect* the opponent to stay consistent with his plan. He won't go out of his way to stop you if doing so would disrupt his own plans too much. Of course, if the two of you are in direct conflict, fighting over exactly the same squares, then you can expect him to do everything possible to foil your strategy: That's Intel and AMD. But more often, even opponents in the same market space will be pursuing different-enough strategies that they will largely ignore the other guy's moves, as Colgate and Procter & Gamble mostly do.

. . . AND THEN FIND A DREAM POSITION

Once the imbalance analysis has been done for you and the other player(s), it's time to ask, Given our "favorable imbalance," what is our dream industry position?

Adobe, Apple, and GE are companies that have gotten a lot of their strategic decisions right. And the reason behind their most successful ones is that they've done what chess players do: imagined a dream position, based on extending their imbalances, and then worked backward.

Many of these successes would not have occurred if traditional planning methods had been used. What would a normal market projection have said about the prospects for the iPod? Based on the then-MP3 market, certainly nothing exciting. Similarly, initial projections for Adobe's PhotoDeluxe were unimpressive, but it became a huge financial and strategic hit. And when GE launched its aircraft engine division, the analysts howled because there were no real projections about future profitability. These CEOs didn't care because they were confident about their ability to see a dream position ahead.

Naturally, this does require one to have a vision of the future, just not one developed by projecting from current numbers. Remember, Grandmasters don't simply try to reason forward from every possible move but, rather, see an attractive position they can develop from their current advantages.

Often in both pursuits, the dream position will be a twist on something one has seen before. According to Nobel economics laureate Herbert Simon, Grandmasters are able to instantly recognize and recall perhaps 50,000 significant patterns, along with key bits of information about typical offensive and defensive play that could result. (This is a big number but maybe not so surprising when you ask yourself how many total faces you might be able to vaguely recognize, along with some feeling about the person.) Interestingly, however, GMs are barely more able than you or I to recognize truly random arrangements of the pieces. Thus, they dig up dream positions by analogizing to a pattern they've seen before.

Great business positions are often concocted in the same way. Back when AOL was still charging per-minute fees, Bob Pittman, president of AOL Networks, envisioned turning AOL's then-existing imbalances into a dream position of generating huge, predictable income streams by imagining it as "Internet access meets magazines," in which content would merit subscription revenues. If he had not had magazine experience, had not "seen it before," he may well not have found the winning plan.

Similarly, we're willing to bet that Steve Jobs' ability to foresee how the iPod could revolutionize the industry was largely driven by his early life experiences with the initial transportable music source that did so, the transistor radio. By traditional measures, the success of the iPod was one of the most unpredictable in retail product history. If you took the previous MP3 market growth trends and projected them forward with a little margin for error, then divided by a realistic market share number for Apple, the answer would have been off by at least two orders of magnitude from the facts. But if you think back to how the first complete solution to portable music, the transistor radio, had reshaped the industry, you could foresee a dream position for a company with Apple's imbalances (software, hardware, distribution, and a customer base: strong imbalances compared with other MP3 companies).

Less dramatic, but just as illustrative, was GE's decision to enter the jet engine business. As their CEO, Jeffrey Immelt, likes to point out, most analysts did not approve of the company's initial investments in airplane engines because hundreds of millions of dollars had to be sunk into very long-range projects with unclear payoffs. But given GE's tremendous expertise in turbine manufacturing and the long-term growth market in airplanes, Immelt could see a dream position for these new products even though he could not provide reliable projections about the size or timing of revenues or profits. The payoff, many years later, has indeed been enormous, and it is now hard to think of GE without that division.

Of course, to imagine a dream position, one also has to have a sense of what trends will develop into meaningful forces and which will be passing fancies. Here Bruce Chizen has a particularly simple and useful rule. If enough big companies are trying to make something happen, it will happen, regardless of all the intelligent reasons why it won't. To him, it was completely obvious that digital photography had to go mainstream, even though industry reports all showed how limited production of liquid crystal displays, inadequate batteries, and a host of other technical problems would retard the process. There were simply too many large companies that had made too many large bets on the segment. As he likes to say, "The laws of capitalism trump the laws of physics."

By the way, when the market is speaking this way, you'd best listen, regardless of your own preconceived notions. Ignoring trends that many large businesses are betting on can result in the business equivalent of getting "posterized," the dread of every NBA player: being the guy getting buried by the superstar's monster dunk in a poster that hangs on every kid's wall. Maybe the most posterized executive is Kenneth H. Olsen, who, as president of Digital Equipment Corporation, said in 1977, "There is no reason for any individual to have a computer in their home." Oops.

Neither Jobs, Chizen, nor Immelt built their successful products through forward numbers projections. They pursued dream positions: Given their positive imbalances, what position could they have in a strategically meaningful market? From that dream position, they worked backward and found a pattern of moves that would get them there. Then they tested the process, calculating through "if-then" tree conjectures to see if one of the moves would lead where they wanted to go, and finally, they "invested" in the strategy by making a move.

Breaking Out of the Box

Our rule that plans must be based on imbalances brings up the subject of "breaking out of the box," one of the most misleading bits of business advice ever doled out. The implication is that companies can simply "whiteboard" new strategies to pursue. But when you're playing chess, you can't just knock the board over and put the pieces back wherever you want—and it's the same with business.

No matter how great that new idea is, plans not based on the imbalances of the position are usually foolish. For proof, let's look at an admittedly fantastic concept but one that the inventors had no right to pursue themselves. Question: Which company thought up the first CAT scanner?

General Electric? Siemens? Nope—although they're good guesses because they're the companies that made all the money in the field. Instead, it was invented at the music company, EMI! One of their researchers, a guy named Godfrey Hounsfield, who later won the Nobel prize for the invention, came up with it. Well, one can understand the desire to monetize such a breakthrough, but licensing it to a company that knew a spinal disc from a compact disc would have been a good idea. It took EMI many years to produce a product and, even though it did work, they had neither the marketing nor manufacturing expertise to make it a hit. Meantime, the two titans entered the fray, with predictable results.

Moral: No matter how wonderful that idea is, if it's unconnected with your imbalances, it's a bad plan.

Back from Dreamland: From There to Here

The next several chapters contain specific chess ideas that have been woven into successful business strategies, so we aren't going to get too detailed yet. Instead, we want to focus on what the key elements of any successful plan are.

Unsurprisingly, the great thinkers about competing organizations before the industrial revolution were military minds. They developed a key set of principles that are relevant to all effective strategies, including those of the chess and business worlds. These folks include Sun Tzu, Machiavelli, Von Clausewitz, and Patton; similar ideas have been espoused by the chess scholars Steinitz, Nimzowitsch, Pachman, and Kasparov. So it's a pretty fair bet that any strategy should pay attention to these points:

1. *Clearly articulate your company's Big Idea.* This most important point seems screamingly obvious but is often botched in practice. Many CEOs wrongly believe that their strategy is well understood by the rest of the organization. There is a good test for this: Can an individual employee guess what the company would expect him to do in making a choice among several alternatives? In general, I think employees at Starbucks, GE, Apple, Adobe, Intel, Google, and Nike could. But at a large percentage of companies, the answer would be, "Not really."

   For example, Motorola's CEO, Ed Zander, has given many speeches saying that the company's "strategy" is to dominate the "convergence" of entertainment devices and computers in consumer living rooms. It sounds good for about 10 seconds, but then the "huh?" sets in. What the heck does that actually mean? Identifying trends is not articulating a strategy.

   Funnily enough, one of the most important points in articulating a clear-enough strategy is being clear about what you *aren't* trying to do. No organization has the resources (or even if it does, the management bandwidth) to contest every square on the board. In a misguided effort to not exclude possibly profitable options, however, most CEOs state their company's goals in ways that are far too general to be meaningful. A crucial part of saying what we want to do is to define what we're not trying to accomplish and what we're going to "allow" our opponents to do. That takes a good player and a strong executive. Personally, I suspect failure to pay attention to this point will lead to significant problems at Google soon enough.

2. *Concentrate forces on an opponent's, or an industry's, weak spot.* This point is discussed in detail in Chapter 9, "Classic Tactics." The crucial idea here is that we have to evaluate an opponent's strengths and weaknesses as much, and as realistically, as we do our own; that's part of the imbalance analysis. Then we have to set our sights on the weak spots, not those that just so happen to be convenient to attack because they suit our "core competency."

3. *Maintain the initiative,* which is also discussed in "Classic Tactics." So long as we dictate the tempo of the action, the opponent won't have time to make the most of what advantages he does have.

4. *Maintain mobility.* This is largely a matter of paying attention to the principles of the "Bad Bishops" and "On the Clock" chapters. Stay light on your feet; don't get your pieces all bollixed up.

5. *Maintain flexibility.* This is the use of that same feedback loop we discussed in "First Mover" and this chapter. It is utterly essential to provide an active method of integrating real-world feedback into your company's plan and adjusting it on the fly.

A BAD PLAN IS BETTER THAN NO PLAN

"Settle on your objective is the rule . . . which one, it matters not. But aimlessly drifting from one to another, this will expose you to strategical disgrace."[8]

The chestnut, a "bad plan is better than no plan," is even truer in business than it is in chess. As discussed in "On the Clock," in our hyperdynamic world, drift is the surest way to fall further behind. Movement itself is good: New skills are learned, new relationships created, new opportunities arise. Morale stays high on a moving ship, but if you get becalmed in the doldrums, watch out for a mutiny.

The single biggest reason that companies freeze up these days is technophobia. They can see profound change on the way and become paralyzed as they try to come up with an ideal response. We know that losing that much time has to be bad (see "On the Clock"), and it is. As the examples below show, it's much better to devise some sort of plan, start moving in that direction, take the feedback, and modify course. *So long as the feedback loop is open and active,* a bad plan is better than no plan.

The contrast between Kodak and Polaroid demonstrates the point nicely. Of course, digital imaging fundamentally threatened both companies. In response, Kodak developed a bad plan; Polaroid, no plan at all.

Kodak set off to conquer the world of digital cameras and, indeed, has captured a big part of the market with a set of pretty good products. In the process, it managed to stay relevant to consumers despite tectonic technology shifts. Now, the only problem with this plan was that competing with Japanese manufacturers in the consumer goods market isn't exactly the best way to healthy profits. This was a most unpleasant realization for a company whose previous business model had enormous gross margins built in. Thus, as related in Chapter 8, "Sac the Exchange!" this plan has hardly made Kodak a big winner; indeed, profits have fallen through the floor in the past few years. But at least it still has a floor to fall through.

Meantime, in pursuing the digital camera market, Kodak developed a capacity for change, attracted fresh blood, learned how to create strategic alliances (previously an unknown idea and one the company was initially bad at), and launched a massive reevaluation of its intellectual property portfolio. This bundle of benefits set the stage for the big exchange sacrifice that it's now playing by moving into printing. Without the changes, information, and cultural shifts generated by its "bad plan," the game would have already been over for Kodak—just like it is for Polaroid. Unable to develop a "perfect plan" to deal with the rapidly changing market, despite constant and ever-more-desperate strategy sessions, Polaroid developed none at all. As new digital technology destroyed its once-secure hold on the film-based instant photography business, Polaroid simply became irrelevant in an extraordinarily short time.

When last seen disappearing into the quicksand, it was still thinking hard, looking for that game-winning move.

A similar example may be found in the war of the worlds between classic media businesses and the new realities of the information economy. Compare the path of the *New York Times* with that of just about any magazine you care to name.

The *Times* began a digital edition in 2001 amid great fear that it would simply cannibalize existing readers without generating any new subscription or advertising revenues. After all, if people could get the same content online for free, would they still pay for a version just to get inky fingertips?

These first halting steps generated unimpressive results, but they led down a road that was absolutely necessary and eventually created great opportunities. Move and things happen. Freeze and they don't.

It sure looked like a bad plan to start. To support its rickety early digital version of the paper, the *Times* faced the question of whether to try to break the bad habit people had of expecting everything on the Internet to be free and charging subscription fees or trying to "monetize eyeballs" (remember that wonderful phrase?) through advertising. They chose the latter, and it didn't work because in the beginning, Internet advertising failed.

After a momentary euphoria at the prospect that "click-throughs" would allow advertisers to understand exactly what their advertising dollars were buying, an ugly truth emerged: not much. Despite the legendary deals that AOL forced down the throats of the dot-com industry, the underlying reality was that Web sites were promising things they couldn't deliver, which, thanks to the miracle of click-through tracking, quickly became patently clear. For publishers who weren't AOL, the money simply did not show up. So the efforts of the *New York Times* to go with the flow looked like folly to many other newspaper guys, who just shook their heads at how such a wonderful company could give away its content for free.

But the *Times* persevered, making one move at a time, probing, improving, adopting to the changes the Internet was bringing to news consumption. Many *Times* readers made www.nyt.com their home page, so they could immediately see *New York Times*–quality news the moment events occurred. More important, the power of the new digital format was used to improve value to readers. For example, an archive search feature was added that obviously was not possible with the print edition. Online readership increased as people got used to the idea and found the electronic features useful. The *Times* found another good move and started offering basic functionality for free but charging for more advanced features.

At the same time, the Internet advertising world started to grow up and got much better at showing advertisers how they got value other than by click-through. Internet penetration and overall digital readership kept increasing. Digital advertising revenues started to climb. More features that helped present the news better (video, audio, high-resolution photography, variable print size) were found, and so were ways of enhancing the online classified ad inventory. Now the *Times* has added free podcasts of digests of the top stories of the day.

Even better, the company now drives off-line subscriptions and advertising with the online content, and vice versa. For example, for those who subscribe for home delivery directly through the *Times* (thus capturing more of the total value chain for the company), several online features that normally require payment are free. The *Times* is finding a laudable balance, putting itself in a position to make the next move, maintaining flexibility, and playing both offense (driving new revenues) and defense (retaining longtime customers despite the "threat" of the Internet).

The most critical point, which cannot be overemphasized, is this: Four years ago, there was no way that the *Times* could have planned to be where it is today. It required making moves, probing and reacting, sticking to its strong squares (highest-quality news reporting), and avoiding disaster. If it had waited for "the answer" to appear, it'd be in a nearly hopeless situation by now. Instead, the *Times*' online revenues are growing at well over 30 percent a year. Not bad for a dinosaur industry.

The need to keep making moves despite uncertainty is not over; it never is. The *Times'* newest challenges are how to address the competition from sophisticated bloggers and "citizen journalists." Just as before, however, instead of hiding from these developments, it's making moves to get in step with them; it's trying to incorporate the work of these "competitors" into its site. The right model hasn't been found yet, but it's still making moves that will position it to be successful. The *Times'* managers are Grandmasters of the information age.

"Oh yeah? Then how come its stock is in the tank?" What!? How can I get heckled in my own book? Oh, sorry, I didn't realize it was you.

Well, here's the story. That's too bad, but it's not a fair critique of the company's reaction to a historic societal disruption. Maybe, like Kodak, the company will never be as profitable as it was or people think it should be. "Unfortunate that is," as Yoda would say, but you have to play the situation that exists on the board currently, not the one you expected or that used to exist. If the analysts would like to repeal the digital revolution, let them; meantime, the company has to do its best to adjust and find new ways forward, and that's what it's doing. Like a Grandmaster who's got a bad position, you have to fight your way out of it one move at a time. Not moving at all while waiting for divine inspiration is certain death (see Chapter 4, "On the Clock," for lots of painful examples).

 LESSONS

1. Plans are essential elements of success, but randomness is an undeniable factor as well. The companies that tend to "get lucky" are the ones that stick to their Big Idea, frequently adjust for exterior conditions, and persevere.
2. Traditional planning methods, based on extrapolating from current trends and picking the largest resulting market to attack, are strategically blind and inherently short-sighted.

3. Commence your strategic planning processes with imbalance analysis, imagine a dream position that could result, and then work backward from there.
4. Make sure the dream position is based on your positive imbalance. Thinking "out of the box" is usually a big mistake.
5. Especially these days, a bad plan really is better than no plan, provided the feedback loop is open and active. So generate a plan and start moving. Waiting for the perfect answer to appear is like waiting for Godot.

CHAPTER SEVEN

STRONG SQUARES

The information age has introduced the greatest business disruptions in history. As on the chessboard, there are now "no lies": Everybody can see everything. The day of the middleman is over. All buyers and sellers can communicate directly with each other, no sources are safe, and all prices are known. Countless companies, and even some whole industries, have evaporated in the light of this sun.

But the flip side of this transparency is the visibility that enables the narrowest businesses to thrive. In particular, the advent of search marketing means that any seller can find any buyer and only has to pay when the potential buyer "proves" her interest with a click. That, plus the ability to hold inventory centrally, cheaply, and often virtually, has created the "long-tail" retail revolution. The "nichiest" niches are viable, even lucrative. Now a Hawaiian natural snacks company can get fat off worldwide wasabi-covered nut sales (Cybersnacks.net) and a tiny family shop in China can direct-market its handmade silk robes globally (chinesemoods.com) and provide great customer service via e-mail, to boot.

Indeed, the trend is even deeper than that. The Web has introduced a fiendish drive for efficient consumption: no waste allowed, no unwanted stuff in with the good bits. Witness the music industry. A decade ago, there was nary a single sold, but the digital revolution has changed everything: Individual tracks now make up about two thirds of all music sales in America. The reason is simply that consumers got tired of being forced to buy an album with 12 bad songs on it just to get the 2 they liked.

All of which makes one of the most classic chess strategies, the idea of "strong squares," more relevant to business today than it ever has been. Strong-square companies make themselves masters of a narrow product or customer niche and then "overprotect" it to make it strong. The result is new sales to old customers, the kind of customer knowledge and relationships that can withstand competitive attack, and eventually, new products and services that conquer adjacent market squares. *The long-tail world creates strong-square opportunities. Grab them!*

Aside from providing new opportunities, strong squares provide an antidote to a world where so much is changing so fast. Now many business gurus preach an ever-more-frenetic response, as if the only way to survive is to change your stripes every year, quarter, or month—to make change itself your core competency. But the companies featured here—like Adobe, ESPN, and even giants like IBM and 3M—show that, aside from being downright exhausting, such an approach is just wrong. You are certainly on the clock, of course, and you do indeed have to move. But those moves are best spent to further develop your strengths, doubling down on the places where you have advantage. The goal is to derive more knowledge and customers from these advantages, to develop and exploit your strong squares.

As John Rice, CEO of the Infrastructure Division of GE, says, as the pace of globalization and technology change increases, "building on past strengths is both harder and more essential than ever before."[1]

SQUARES AND PIECES

Before we get to our main topic, let's first understand a critical difference in the way that beginners and experts look at a chessboard. What novices see is a tangle of Knights and Bishops, pawns and Rooks. They try to figure out what's about to take what. From their point of view, all the "action" is at the piece level.

When Grandmasters look at a chessboard, they see something completely different: the squares themselves. Maybe there are pieces on them, maybe not, but they see the fight as one to control squares: lines of them in any direction (diagonals, files, and ranks), color complexes (light or dark), or even, as we'll see in this chapter, just one single square. The pieces are means of controlling space, not ends in themselves.

Businesspeople exhibit a similar dichotomy. Average executives see products to push, attack, and defend; great executives see markets to control.

At the typical company, meetings about increasing revenues focus on attacking a competitor's product (his pieces) or pushing the existing product (our pieces) into a new market. This works infrequently because such thinking is all about the "pieces," the products themselves, and not about creating the sorts of answers for underlying customer needs that would yield market control. Peter Drucker would call this selling (attacking or pushing products) rather than marketing (targeting market space by developing products to satisfy consumer demands).

We can see the difference clearly by comparing Apple and Sony, an interesting pair because they both have long histories of creating cool electronics, and they have two of the great brands in the world. Their parallels, and currently very different trajectories, speak volumes about the right way to look at a business chessboard.

First, let's reflect on Sony's unprecedented 30-year run at innovating products that became runaway hits (a record that Apple is now chasing). What was behind the first transistor radio, the first portable television, early videocassette players, the Walkman, and the 3.5-inch floppy disk? More than anything else, it was that Sony's amazing founder, Akio Morita, along with a close team of advisors, spent huge amounts of time simply trying to understand what consumers were trying to do with electronics. Their goal was to use their expertise to deliver simple-to-use products that met unaddressed customer needs. They succeeded spectacularly, over and over again (if that sounds like the modern Apple, there's a reason).

LOOKING AT THE SAME BOARD, SONY SEES THIS:

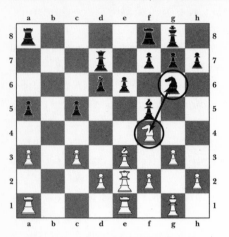

SONY LOOKS AT THE PIECES FIRST; IT
WORRIES ABOUT HOW ITS KNIGHT IS
ATTACKING THE OTHER ONE, AND BEING
ATTACKED AT THE SAME TIME . . .

. . . BUT GRANDMASTER APPLE SEES THIS:

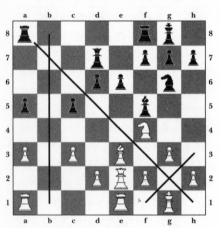

APPLE SEES MARKET OPPORTUNITY FIRST:
THE LONG DIAGONAL, THE OPEN "B" FILE,
AND THAT JUICY "X" AROUND THE
WHITE KING. IT DEPLOYS ITS PIECES
TO CONTROL THOSE SQUARES.

He was an incredible player, a guy who could see market squares and conquer them.

That incredible run more or less ended in the early eighties, when Morita let go of the product innovation and launch process. Since then, Sony's product development process has become dominated by internal competition among scores of development teams. Each is pushing a design based on outflanking a competitive product's feature set or on "productizing" an engineering brainstorm. It is, essentially, an invention contest largely judged by marketing experts and financial types, who then look to push the winning pieces toward becoming products.

Sony's recent problems reflect the change in its board vision. It used to see market squares; now it sees product pieces. The result is many fantastic novelties, like the Aibo robotic dog, that have absolutely no natural market. ELO points are how Grandmasters are rated and ranked; Sony has lost a ton of them lately.

When Steve Jobs taught himself business chess, you can imagine he studied "Morita's greatest games." He plays precisely the same style, applying his company's expertise to provide consumers elegant, easy-to-use products that do things consumers actually want done. He is completely focused on finding the squares and then controlling them, not just pushing his company's pieces around.

In fact, he has improved on the great master's play by extending the "understand-the-customer" mantra to an entirely new level. It seems that every single employee at Apple knows who its customer is and what that customer wants. They design products to take control of a file or diagonal, a specific set of connected market squares: young users, graphics professionals, people who want computers to be simple and easy.

When Apple thinks about how cool a product would be, they're thinking about how it would satisfy market needs, not how novel or sleek it is (sure, that the products also look good helps, but that's secondary; their competitors make tons of attractive disasters). Apple understands the squares it's after and then finds a "piece" to control them, whether that's a brand new appliance, like the iPhone, or just an intuitive application that makes common tasks easier, like iMovie. Apple focuses on the squares.

Perhaps the most amazing single aspect of this approach, though, is how Apple has been able to extend it to the retail space. Here again, the comparison with Sony is telling.

Apple was pushed to open the Apple stores by the realization that the Best Buys of the world would never be able to display and explain Apple's products as anything other than just another computer; it was effectively forced into it to keep the basic value proposition intact. It started with a mock-up in a warehouse near the Apple campus but recognized that the first try was all wrong: The merchandise was laid out by product category (all the laptops were stacked together, as is typical in stores), not by customer needs (how the products could be used to solve different problems: video capture and editing, for example). So it tore down the first try and reorganized so that products were grouped by what problems they solved for the consumer, a retail space manifestation of its design principles. And the coup de grace in user-friendliness was the "genius bar" in the back, where customers could get all the advice—and repair services—they need.

Compare this approach with Sony's "style stores": attractive, sleek, sort of a fashion house for their products. Indeed, that's what they were designed to be: a showcase. But showcases don't solve problems; they push product pieces. Indeed, it is difficult to get quality advice from the Sony personnel about how to hook up its premium equipment (an unthinkable occurrence at an Apple store), although they certainly do look good in that all-black.

The results are in, and Apple is now the world champion of retailing. Its stores generate by far the most dollars per square foot of retail space in the country, outstripping Tiffany by more than 50 percent and other electronics outlets by 400 percent and more, according to one report by Sanford Bernstein. Sony is a blip too small to measure.

Thinking about this, I can't help but fantasize about a Jobs-versus-Kasparov match-up.

JUST ONE?

Now that we see the basic way Grandmasters think about squares, we're ready to take the idea to its logical extreme: the strategy of pursuing mastery over a single one.

The great Argentinean Grandmaster Aaron Nimzowitsch first described strong-square theory in his famous book *My System* in 1925. He advanced the then-radical, now-commonplace, idea that a winning position can be constructed off control of a single square, if you overprotect it to make it strong. The critical idea is to get uncontestable control of a space, no matter how narrow, so overwhelming that the opponent can't realistically think about taking it back.

OK, but then what? True, you can't exactly claim checkmate just yet, but you are on the way. To start, that square can be a permanent roost for one of your powerful pieces so that it can radiate its power over the board: A Knight roosted deep in enemy territory on a strong square is a virtual win. You can also use strong squares as secure central dispatch points from which to launch successive pieces into a contested area: a chess shuttle-stop. In chess, and in business, *the owner of the strong square can keep "going back to the well" to bring more forces to bear.* As a result, control of a tiny board niche, one single square, can lead to a winning game.

Remember, just occupying a square is not enough. As Nimzowitsch asked, "in a battle, if I seize a bit of land with a handful of soldiers, without having done anything to prevent enemy bombardment of the position, would it ever occur to me to speak of a conquest of the terrain in question? Obviously not."[2]

Instead, you have to overinvest resources in the square, lock it away in the family vault. *It is this overinvestment in existing business that has allowed companies featured here to thrive and expand.* By overprotecting their markets and customers, they drive not just dependable revenue streams but also product development efforts, new customer acquisition, and ultimately, control over adjacent markets.

Today, Nimzowitsch would be a welcome guest at Wharton. Our one-to-one, long-tail, information economy has made his strategy more relevant than ever. And it's because the most important part of the "information economy" is the information about what customers really need and want and where *they* see the future. These companies find their product improvements and business development ideas inside their customer relationships, and it's from this base that they derive ever more income from their market squares.

What Is a Business Strong Square?

Business strong squares are tightly defined market niches in which *a company is the best there is.* This is not a "core competency," which is merely what the company happens to be best at. The difference is absolutely fundamental. Strong-square strategy demands that you *control* some niche, *no matter how narrow.* If you don't have one, get one.

Let's name some. Technology does not count, but graphics software (Adobe) does, as does small business accounting software

(Intuit). Food is a no, but sauce (Tabasco) is a yes. Home improvement? Uh-uh. Paints (Sherwin Williams)? Sure. Sports apparel? Nope. Professional athletic performance apparel (Under Armor)? Definitely. Burglar alarms? Well, maybe; but car theft prevention (Lojack), certainly.

Among winning companies, the trend is pervasive: Take a look at successful airlines (Southwest), chocolate makers (Godiva), even underwear sellers (Victoria's Secret). Each has a readily identifiable niche in their industry. Don't buy garden pots, buy exclusive handmade Italian terra cotta (Seibert and Rice). Macy's is out; Williams-Sonoma is in.

Service industries are the same. Being a general law firm is not a strong square, but being the leading asbestos litigation firm counts. (Interestingly, one of them holds the record for how much they'll pay Google to be listed at the top of the search results: "asbestos litigation" costs them about $25 each time someone clicks on their name, which shows how profitable acquiring a potential litigant must be. But *please* don't think about taking out your frustration with lawyers by hitting that link all day.) A travel agent who can bill herself as the ultimate expert on Peru does well, but the generalists in her office are now out selling real estate. Even the better hospitals are advertising themselves as specialists in cancer care, sports medicine, childbirth, or cosmetic surgery.

Bruce Chizen, the CEO who lead Adobe to greatness, is a strong-square master. He has turned a niche focus into one of the largest software companies in the world. And he's using a strong-square approach to both expand and defend the company's turf.

The company established its niche with PostScript, which offered a remarkable breakthrough back in the day: Different fonts could be faithfully generated from one printer. That led to a deep understanding of other digital image issues, like those involved in pictures. Photoshop became a flagship, a product that thoroughly dominates its market of high-end artists and designers; there really is no other product that serious pros consider. As the Internet became ever more part of the life of such folks, the company kept pace with their needs, eventually resulting in the purchase of Macromedia for its

"Flash" product line. (That acquisition, by the way, was a model for such things: The expertise, product lines, customer sets, and culture of Macromedia echoed Adobe's, and the integration was smooth and rapid. Companies competing for the same strong squares are much more likely to create a successful merger than most.) Along the way, a version of PostScript for the information age, aka Acrobat, was born from this digital graphics strong square.

The exploitation of the Photoshop franchise is particularly instructive. By the company's own admission, this product, if incredibly powerful, is also complex and hard to use. It sells for nearly a thousand dollars and, therefore, provides excellent margins, but its target market is limited to a few million users.

Many companies would, therefore, have gone off to find new products with broader reach. Instead, Chizen found new markets from his existing square.

When PhotoDeluxe was launched, many thought it was a big mistake: The market was small; popular digital cameras of the day produced grainy, low-resolution images that were hardly worth cleaning up; and only a few brave souls knew how to get the pictures from their cameras and into their computers anyway. On top of everything else, why risk "cannibalizing" the superhigh-margin Photoshop with a low-end product? But as usually happens with strong squares, the company's existing strength helped create its own new market, and consumer imaging has become a company mainstay. And by going deep into its strong square this way, Adobe has prevented others from "attacking the base of its pawn chain" (see Chapter 9, "Classic Tactics") and seizing a foothold in its markets.

Chizen never forgets Nimzowitsch's rule that strong squares require constant overprotection. And he knows how to attack when a competitor does.

Quark dominated the world of publishing software for more than a decade. It had a ubiquitous product protected by high switching barriers: Both publishers and designers would have to switch—at the same time, and to the same product—for Quark to lose its position. Forget strong, that's indomitable! But they blew it anyway by ignoring the most important aspect of the strategy, customer relationships. The dominant position led to insensitivity to changing user needs, poor customer service, and the belief that any pricing strategy for updates could succeed.

This created a "love the product, hate the company" mind-set among its users. Well, thought Chizen, if they aren't going to protect it, let's take it. Adobe bought PageMaker, a small product in the space, to gain the expertise and rewrote the code to mesh with Adobe's product line. Adobe attacked at both the publisher level, convincing one or two leading publishers to switch, and at the designer level by propagating the tool through schools with ultralow prices. Both sets of users loved InDesign, a product that worked perfectly with Photoshop, Acrobat, Illustrator, and Flash and that was being sold by a company they genuinely liked. InDesign is now the leading force in the industry. The story of Quark is an ideal example of what happens when you stop paying attention to your strong square; Adobe's is a story of how to leverage a strong square into more board space.

Adobe's success in the turbulent technology market is a testimony to the power of the strategy, but ESPN's success in the even more chaotic media space might be more impressive still. The funny thing is, these days one can actually wonder whether "sports media" is narrow enough to be considered a strong square, but there was no debate about this back in 1979, when it had to fill airtime with tractor pulls.

After years of painstakingly developing programming to establish a solid lineup (including, I'm happy to say, the "Intel World Chess Grand Prix"), ESPN slowly expanded to a second channel of programming, then a third, just delivering sports news, and then a fourth for college sports. Now, its family of channels is the linchpin in any cable TV distribution deal.

Seeing this growth out of one strong square, of continually reinvesting in your niche, is an important lesson. But the most instructive aspect of ESPN's strategy is the way it has moved its strong-square relationships across delivery platforms, a model for today's threatened traditional media companies.

First, it went from TV to print, attacking the king of sports magazines, *Sports Illustrated*. Like Nimzowitsch using his strong square as a launching pad for a mate, ESPN attacked directly from its sports TV base: It marketed the magazine on TV, got its stars to write columns, and kept the same super-insider hip style. Essentially, *ESPN started to sell the same customer set a different product,* rather than simply going after the more general sports fan market or even the *Sports Illustrated* circulation base. In this way, its own strong square assured its success in a way much more fundamental than simply extending a popular brand name. Many others had taken on *SI* and failed; ESPN succeeded because it first established its own adjacent strong square and kept drawing from it to build the new business.

The company also beat *Sports Illustrated* to the Web and created a far more robust offering for avid sports fans. *Sports Illustrated* essentially outsourced Web development to CNN—not exactly a natural combination—and wound up with a very average site that showed, and gained, little insight into sports fans' psyches. ESPN, conversely, poured tremendous focus and resources into its site and delivered numerous innovations: all sorts of advanced, up-to-the-second virtual game coverage; "ESPN Motion," one of the first Web video services featuring its own highlights; and cutting-edge fantasy sites for all major sports. This forged yet another level of involvement and understanding of its customer base.

Now it's being converted to the "third screen," mobile devices. Unlike most companies chasing this rainbow, ESPN has a strong square to base this attack from. Its Web site, in particular, is a great source of information about what its users are most interested in. For example, the company will also be able to match users from Web to phone and automatically deliver mobile content based on, for example, the teams and players the user has checked out most while at the ESPN site. Already it claims more users for its mobile-phone Web site than most normal Web sites have, and many tens of thousands of fans have registered for frequent e-mail and IM updates.

Indeed, John Zehr, an SVP at ESPN, puts it this way: "You start to learn more and more about your fans as they migrate from platform to platform . . . what we're really doing now is customer relationship management."[3] That is a very fair summary of strong-square strategy in the information revolution.

Like any player, ESPN has made its share of mistakes. It forgot its own lesson for a bit when it came to international programming. ESPN got carried away with pushing its big piece, "Sportscenter," and forgot the squares, what foreign sports fans wanted. Thus, when it went to expand into those markets, ESPN initially created one show with highlights from all around the world, localized only by voice-overs in a dozen or so different languages. It failed: Mysteriously, people in Kenya just didn't care about bobsledding action from Canada. But ESPN did wake up and got serious about localizing to meet customer interests. Now, in Latin America, it covers soccer, soccer, and a little baseball; in Australia and New Zealand, it covers rugby and Australian-rules football. It was more expensive to do it this way, of course; but delivering what customers actually want, rather than what you have to sell them, gets rewarded: revenues and profits have started to escalate dramatically.

Now, perhaps you think this whole strong-squares strategy is not so brilliant. But here's the mistake ESPN didn't make: It didn't suddenly believe it understood TV watchers and go on to create programming for a "broader audience," a mistake repeated countless times in countless industries. It knew it understood sports fans, and it put 100 percent of its energy into that then-narrow niche. In accordance with the theory, this approach has proved an endless source of revenues and customers.

Although the information revolution has elevated the importance of this strategy, it's been a successful one for a long time. Back in the 1920s, just as Nimzowitsch was writing, a company with a single product, sandpaper, had its workers out visiting car manufacturers who were preparing their cars for painting. The reps noticed how much trouble their customers had making the popular new two-toned vehicles; the paints kept running over each other. Watching this, a guy named Richard Drew suddenly realized that a strip of the paper (without the sand) could cover one color while the other was applied and suggested to his boss that they put a little adhesive on one side to facilitate this. Masking tape was born, and 3M was on its way.

Drew applied his insight again a couple of years later. When cellophane became a popular way of wrapping meats and bakery items, Drew saw that the same adhesive-on-one-side approach could be used as a waterproof way of sealing these packages and, voilà! Scotch Tape. The Great Depression made the inexpensive product into the fix-it solution for everything from window shades to shoes and luggage. The product became a staple. Needless to say, there would be no way to design a research project that would ultimately have produced anything so useful. But real-world customer knowledge, strong-square strategy, could.

Well, OK, these are cute stories, but can 3M, a company with several tens of thousands of products, be said to have a strong-square strategy? The answer is yes because the vast majority of the company's products are applications of the company's core coating and bonding technologies, just like its tapes and Post-It notes are. The combination of specific technical skills and a deep understanding of customer needs is a winning plan even at the biggest companies.

As 3M shows, a beauty of strong-square strategy is that we can always make a move and know it's going to be a pretty good one. The strategy does not ask for, or require, blinding insights and massive market leaps. Simple overprotection can make some pretty amazing things happen.

NEW SQUARES ON THE BOARD

For early-stage ventures, the big news is that strong-square strategy works better in the information age than ever before. Look at Zappos.com, for example. At the turn of the century, many would have thought that trying to compete with a behemoth like Amazon would be foolish. Many more thought that trying to sell such an obviously returnable item as shoes was doomed. But Zappos feared not, figuring, rightly, that the very "problem" of selling shoes over the Web would render footwear a strong square.

Zappos developed an extremely user-friendly return system and then added a feedback feature that provides some great, shoe-specific advice from other users (such as, "77 percent of customers report this shoe feels about half a size larger than labeled"). By incorporating that feature, Zappos is capturing some of the network effect discussed earlier: the bigger the user base, the deeper the pool of advice on any given shoe. It has settled on a nice, simple presentation of the shoes from any angle so people know what they're buying. Throw in great selection and pricing, and it's a hit. Customer satisfaction runs high, and word-of-mouth marketing is driving rapid growth.

Off line, UnderArmor is also an instructive example. In the mid-nineties, no one would have thought there was a need for another sportswear company; Nike, Adidas, and a host of small fry were already filling sales racks to the brim.

But from his perspective as a football player at the University of Maryland, Kevin Plank saw an important uncontrolled square. All his T-shirts simply absorbed and held onto all that sweat at the two-a-days; not only was it messy, but by keeping the moisture next to his skin, the shirts actually kept the sweat from doing its job and cooling him down. Surely something better could be invented? Yes, it could. He developed a rapid-wicking material and sold the shirts to several hot-weather teams almost immediately. And by sticking to the high-end professional-quality market he knew personally, he was able to beat out Nike for control of this profitable square.

IDENTIFYING YOUR STRONG SQUARE

Remember, strong squares aren't necessarily what you do best. They're where you have a distinct advantage over the rest of the market. Many companies have core competencies; few have strong squares.

The search for your strong square is often a subtle exercise. For example, you might well say that Amazon's strong square is selling retail products on line or, more specifically, selling books online. But if that's what you think, you'll have to convince Jeff Bezos.

Indeed, Amazon's lead in e-tailing is under fierce attack from more traditional merchants, like Wal-Mart and Target. Logically enough, as time goes by and more people go online, the typical Web customer looks more and more like the typical bricks-and-mortar customer. And you know where they shop. Over the past few years, the traditional retailers have largely caught up with the early Web birds, just in time to take advantage of the fact that their customers are arriving online in droves. Amazon still holds a lead with young, tech-savvy users, but they are shrinking as a percentage of online buyers. For a company that needs to show big growth to Wall Street, that's not good news.

Nonetheless, Bezos thinks he has a strong square to exploit: not e-tailing itself but, rather, the infrastructure that underlies it. He's reinvesting heavily in that area, but not just to sell more books and electronics; instead, he's offering up these leading-edge capacities directly to other businesses. For example, developers can tap directly into Amazon's superpowerful computers and use them like time-share condos. Companies can use the equivalent of an Amazon self-storage service to archive their data instead of buying their own expensive servers (obviously, there's a huge economy of scale involved). Young companies can also use it to get their businesses launched.

So, he's identified the one thing that Amazon's better at than anyone, and even though it's an unusual square, he's heavily reinvesting in it, and he's going to make this the cornerstone of his game. Play like him.

And not, for example, like Ted Gates. He somehow wound up thinking that Gateway's strong square was home electronics, and he tried to expand into all sorts of items unconnected to the company's strengths by licensing out the name and opening a chain of "home stores." It's as though he was a bad contestant on the old "$20,000 Pyramid": He thought the category was "things that plug in" when it was really "building computers to order." (The only guys he beat on the show were the marketing geniuses who tried to remake Las Vegas into a family resort a few years ago.) Eventually Gates lost his seat at the table when Acer bought the company. Strong-square strategy is powerful, indeed, but you need to know which one you're after.

THE GREATEST PLAYER IN HISTORY?

We'll finish this chapter with a look at Western Union, for here is a company we can all take our hats off to. Rather than being overcome by waves of earthshaking communications technology changes, it has thrived for more than 150 years by sticking to a strong-square strategy.

Initially, of course, Western Union was purely a telegraph company, one so famous that its name was synonymous with the product: "Sir, a Western Union has just arrived for you!" Fairly early on, however, the company recognized the value of using its network to transfer money by wire, probably just as startling a marketing claim when first introduced as "pause live TV" was for TiVo.

Over the 150 years, Western Union simply never allowed technology shifts to get in the way of its real business, individual communications and money transfers. Its ability to understand its customer and adjust its offerings with changes in communications technology is simply amazing. After all, you have to know something about your target audience to invent the idea of a singing telegram!

This deep customer understanding has always been paired with a willingness to embrace change and play the sacrifice rather than cling to an old model. Both elements are evident in Western Union's impressive list of "firsts": the first company to have a transcontinental telephone line, to introduce a stock ticker, to provide a standard time service, to provide a consumer credit card, to have an intercity fax service (in 1935!), and to use microwave relay stations instead of fixed wires. It had the first U.S. commercial communications satellite (Westar I) and was the first in the United States to offer prepaid phone cards. It did have a brief stint in bankruptcy, but that was due to financial mismanagement, not a lack of customers or revenues. Today, its business prospects remain bright: It has more than 250,000 offices around the globe and is ideally positioned to provide financial services (especially international money transfers, of course) to the vast number of the world's unbanked.

Western Union has been successful because it leveraged its customer knowledge to cope with technology change and stay in synch with its users, morphing its methods and business models to deliver a basic service that has changed little in all that time.

All this is certainly not to say that Western Union never blundered. Because the technology was not useful for its business of long-distance communications, it rejected that minor invention of Alexander Graham Bell's. Initial telephone technology permitted communication over a maximum of three miles, so it didn't fit the model. Oh, well. All players make mistakes. But the successful ones stick to their strong squares and win anyway.

In my own start-up, we had, as you know, initially made the traditional rookie business mistake of confusing a cool technology for a business. For years, we hung on by our fingernails, looking for a square we could dominate with our great 3D graphics technology. Then we made the critical discovery: AOL, by far the largest ISP of the day, had been around so long (by Internet standards) that its client-side software did not support the graphics capabilities necessary to deliver rich media ads to its customers. Boy, did that look like a strong square to grab!

Focusing on it made the company. It was tough going at first; I can still remember the stinging rebuke of one executive after our first pitch: "You guys talked a Cadillac to get in here but showed us a Chevy." But we kept after it and agreed to make several changes to our software that would make it work better with AOL's system. This was the beginning of a wonderful co-design process that would wed us over the long term. Eventually, it needed our rich media function so much that it embedded our software inside its core software client, giving us the mass distribution and credibility we needed.

The relationship led to a deep understanding of the ad-serving industry and what it needed. And with the knowledge and experience we gained, we were able to design products and services that we could sell to both AOL and other companies in the Internet advertising world. We wound up building an entire business off that square.

At the end of the day, then, by overprotecting our strong square, we got new ones. And that's the idea.

LESSONS

1. Remember that you're fighting to control a market, not simply trying to outfeature some other product. Look at the squares first, then the pieces.

2. Focus your efforts on a narrow niche to dominate; these days, it's almost impossible to be too narrow, so long as there are some paying customers somewhere in the world. The information revolution has effectively created more squares on the board; go get one.

3. Overprotect the square: keep investing in it with the particular goal of understanding the customers' needs as deeply as possible. Put your best people on your strongest relationships, not your newest ones.

4. Don't confuse your delivery method with your strong-square advantage; follow (or even pull!) your customers to new platforms.

5. Maintain your grip. Do not stretch your organization in a way that weakens control of the strong square, no matter how attractive the short-term economics appear to be. Remember Gateway but don't emulate it.

Chapter Eight

Sac the Exchange!

No company is immune to the continuing cycle of market formation and destruction. But it's almost unfair how the information revolution has accelerated the process. Ask Michael Dell: Even the best business models have an ever-shorter life span. What's a company to do?

One good idea is to try what chess players often do when an idea begins to run out of steam: an exchange sacrifice. As you can guess from the name, this requires swapping something more valuable for something less valuable. Why would you do that? Because you create some new, dynamic opportunities in the bargain. You are converting one sort of advantage into an entirely different kind. It's a little like converting mass into energy: You create a lot of heat and light when some of the material disappears.

Similarly, when business models begin to lose steam, product innovation is just not enough; simply pushing the pieces around won't do. Reinventing the basic method of doing business is frequently the only way forward, and that typically involves forgoing "sacrificing" current revenues to create new opportunities.

The most important point to understand about an exchange sacrifice is that you're *converting* one sort of advantage (a nice Rook for a mere Knight or Bishop) to achieve another one (holes we can infiltrate around the White King). It's not a crazy desperation move, but rather an attempt to "liberate" and exploit advantages before they dissipate. In this chapter, we'll see how several leading companies have done just that.

THE TRICK IS KNOWING WHEN

First, though, we need to ask, When is it time to start looking for an exchange sacrifice? Often, deteriorating performance of a unit can be chalked up to poor execution, seasonality, or some other temporary phenomenon that will pass or that can be fixed by internal adjustments. No dramatic sacrifice is needed.

But if that positive imbalance that you identified in "bad plans" starts to slip away, it might be time for something dramatic. The advice is the opposite of your mom's warning about riding that bike: Don't lose your imbalance!

So it's time to look for a sac when (1) competitors have pretty good luck replicating your previously superior business model (Dell and Wal-Mart); (2) new, lower-cost competitors have arrived (Xerox facing Canon, or Intel back when it made DRAM chips, similarly facing attack by less-expensive Japanese competitors); (3) commoditization threatens the basic way you extract value from your market (IBM); (4) other business models are making yours obsolete (AOL, faced with the emergence of free ISPs); (5) new technologies threaten your core business (Kodak and Western Union); or (6) superior delivery models for the same product appear (the newspaper and TV industries, looking at the Internet).

You'll note that some of the companies just mentioned have been extremely successful while some are in deep trouble. The former group played an exchange sacrifice when they saw trouble for their imbalance; the others tried to hang onto a dwindling advantage too long.

What is required, once you see the old model begin to lose its edge, is a way to convert it into a different *kind* of advantage while it still retains most of its power. You need to do it while you can still get something different and valuable back. The longer you wait, the less you'll see in return.

How It Works

Let's see how it works in a game. Don't worry about whether you understand the following terminology; it really doesn't matter. What matters is that you understand how a player exchanges one kind of advantage for another kind of advantage as the game goes along.

Say a player starts out with e4 and his opponent replies with the Pirc defense: solid, but one that offers White a significant space advantage in the middle of the board. Using that spatial edge, White might be able to create a situation in which his Bishops have more mobility than his opponent's and are therefore more potent than his. So the "spatial advantage" turns into a "minor-piece advantage." And perhaps these active Bishops become so strong that Black is forced to sacrifice a pawn to force a trade and get rid of one of them. So now the minor-piece advantage has become a "material advantage." Very good, but far from checkmate. So then the player needs to find a different plan, perhaps one that clears a path down the board and turns the extra pawn into a Queen. Finally, with so much extra firepower, the player can turn his attention to a direct assault on the enemy King and deliver a checkmate.

So you can see that players are forced to continuously trade the *kind* of advantage they have in order to win: space for material, material for time, static for dynamic. It's not just that trades are made, it's that the fundamental nature of the two elements of the bargain is different.

Come to think of it, that's no real surprise: You rarely spend money to buy money; instead, you convert it into something totally different, like a TV. A chess advantage is like having money to spend on something. A business advantage is, too. Exchange sacrifices are just a clear way of illustrating the idea.

A Few Nice Moves . . .

An excellent example is the way AOL exchanged its subscription model for a strictly ad-based approach. Interestingly, it's actually the second time in the game they've sacrificed the exchange.

Everybody knows that AOL paved the way for the onlining of America through an old-fashioned dial-up service. (What most people don't remember is that their breakthrough feature was chat rooms, a big improvement over the previous "bulletin board" functions of other rudimentary online services. Ironically, given that "adult content" is the early driver of almost all entertainment technology, AOL would today block the content that drove the success of their breakthrough feature.) At that point, AOL charged by the minute and kept that model as it became a more general content provider with its "walled garden" and limited Web access. This model served it well for a long time and even brought all sorts of third-party providers to the party: for example, AOL would share the revenues generated by online play with the game developers.

The first time AOL played a business model exchange sacrifice was in 1996. It could see that its per-minute model was stalling new user growth as other ISPs charged into the game. So it took a gamble and went to an all-you-can-eat monthly charge, even though this was certain to diminish revenues from its heaviest users.

In the short term, this move created operational havoc. AOL suffered serious service interruptions for some time and even had to resort to kicking its former best customers, the "excessive" users, off line to clear capacity for its swamped dial-up system. Indeed, it was frequently difficult for users to even get an active line (the idea that you could get a busy signal while attempting to connect to the Internet is a source of astonishment to teenagers). In the long run, though, the subscription model was far more palatable for most users, and subscriber growth exploded. Within a few years, AOL had on the order of 30 million users.

This revenue model, at its height, generated upwards of $10 billion a year. That, my friend, is one hell of a recurring cash flow, a heroin habit that few could kick.

But two problems developed. The first and most serious one was that, in the end, open systems always beat closed systems (see Chapter 9, "Classic Tactics"), and the Internet is the ultimate open system. Try as it might to make the walled garden of AOL content worthy of a big subscription fee, its Adam and Eve users wanted to taste more knowledge than was offered inside AOL's safe confines, and indeed, off they went. Soon, the couple discovered that there was no need to pay for garden entrance if you were just going to leave anyway. Cheaper, no-frills dial-up services began to eat away at subscriber growth.

At the same time, the promise of interactive advertising began to catch on and to generate enough revenue for sites to put up great content without charging subscription fees. The idea that you could "monetize eyeballs," a rallying cry in the run-up to the great tech bubble, finally started to come true. Of course, AOL wanted to capitalize on this phenomenon, too, so it rolled out a huge advertising sales force to do so.

But, but, but. At bottom, making money this way fundamentally conflicted with the company's subscription model; executives on the content side used to gripe that the interactive guys wanted to make the whole service into "one bad ad." Meantime, the ad guys couldn't get cooperation from the content side to place ads in the most trafficked areas or to integrate sponsorships and promotions in ways that could be packaged for big money. Worse, the slow deterioration of the user base, brought on by high subscription fees, limited the number of users to whom ads could be shown and, hence, the ad revenues that could be derived.

With competition from low-cost ISPs, portals like Yahoo!, and broadband springing up everywhere, subscribers started bailing in droves. The model had seen its best days but was still producing some mighty fine numbers.

So here was a classic chess moment. There is a beautiful asset, still a $7 billion revenue stream. But the game had bogged down, and something new needed to be done. It was a decent but far from certain bet that if subscription fees were dropped, usership would increase, thus, presumably, increasing advertising revenues. But it was all a guess. So management, to its credit, "played the sac"; it made all of AOL's key features free and stopped selling subscriptions.

And, the results have made the chess world smile. In the first quarter of 2007, the AOL unit of TimeWarner reported a 27 percent increase in profits, despite a 25 percent dip in revenues and, of course, the expected big drop in subscribers. The exchange cost material but created opportunities that can carry the company into the next phase of the game.

The point: *AOL found a new way to take advantage of that huge user base before it lost it.* As you can see from this example, the sacrifice isn't an abandonment of a strength; it's a conversion, a different way to exploit it.

Note that we've been talking about the online operations here, not the consequences of the TimeWarner merger. On that subject, however, a modest prediction: Having had a rough go in the opening, TimeWarner may still turn out a winner in the endgame. As online advertising becomes more brand oriented and less of a direct-marketing effort, the blend of the TimeWarner media properties and AOL's reach will become more important. The big advertisers, like Procter & Gamble, haven't really shown up to the Internet party yet; when they do, they'll want to integrate with media properties. Moreover, AOL's recent moves have finally given it the necessary advertising technologies and infrastructure to pull that off.

Contrast the idea of an exchange sacrifice to the alternative, simply selling off a line of business to raise cash and then using the proceeds to buy in an unrelated business. No matter how attractive the new business might be, such a move creates many of its own problems, and it's well known that the vast majority of mergers fail. In many ways, an exchange sacrifice can be a safer bet; rather than trying to create an advantage completely out of the blue, it is a transformation, a reuse, a morphing of an old advantage into a new one.

A telling statistic comes from Chris Zook, author of the *From the Core* series.[1] He says that four out of five successful regeneration stories involve companies exploiting existing strengths, uncovering assets and using them in a new way. That shows the power of exchange sacrifices that re-lever existing assets. Sometimes the moves are hard to find because the assets turn up in various forms: intellectual property, business platforms, distribution systems, or underexploited infrastructure. The trick is to change the way your advantages are being utilized.

It's important to remember that whether an exchange sacrifice is a good move or not is not necessarily determined by whether it's ultimately successful. These ideas don't always work even when they're the best alternative available. They always involve risk, but they're still better than just waiting around while the clock runs to zero. For example, as of this writing, we don't know whether the bold and interesting exchange sacrifice being played by Kodak will work; but we definitely give it an "!," the chess symbol for an especially good move.

Kodak was one of the greatest businesses of the twentieth century for three reasons. First, its products and services were of untouchable quality. Second, they were constantly used up, so consumers had to buy more. Third, the products had amazing profit margins built in. No wonder the company squinted through the haze of the technology revolution and hoped that the digital stuff was a mirage.

But dutifully if not enthusiastically, Kodak responded, using a powerful engineering culture to crank out a credible line of digital cameras that, to the surprise of some analysts, did manage to capture market share from the likes of Sony and Minolta. The problem was, competing with those companies in a hardware business meant that there would be revenues but little profit. Now what?

It took a new CEO, Antonio Perez, to find a decent move in this position. And it was an exchange sac. In rummaging through Kodak's extensive intellectual property portfolio, Perez discovered some powerful technology for making better, cheaper inks for home photo printing. Kodak's inks are pigment-based, so they hold their color for many more years than traditional dyes, and in their intellectual property were ways to make the colors as vibrant as any dye on the market.

So the trade was an old business in creating images for a new one, film for ink. A meaningful percentage of Rochester, New York, was laid off, and the marketing and research budgets for the traditional businesses were slashed. All the energy was put into a new line of play.

This exchange sacrifice also exploits a key chess rule: As explained later, you can't just attack anywhere you want; you have to attack a weakness. And the weakness of mighty Hewlett-Packard is the price that consumers pay for replacement ink cartridges. Kodak claims it will cut the cost of printing images by half compared with existing printers.

HP has intentionally established a system by which printers are cheap and inks are expensive. To date, this has worked well largely because no one has attacked it, and competitors just replicate the strategy with smaller market share. So, you might say, HP will simply reduce its margins and head Kodak off at the pass. But maybe not. The HP system has an inherent disadvantage that Kodak is also exploiting and that makes a higher price for HP replacement cartridges somewhat unavoidable: In the HP system, the consumer is always buying a new printer head on top of the ink cartridge. In the Kodak system, the ink jets themselves are not swapped out every time a consumer's kid has printed too many pages of her artwork.

It is important to note something here: Kodak might not win this game anyway. Early reviews of the Kodak printers were good but not outstanding. HP is a fearsome competitor with enormous resources and a deeply ingrained industry position. They certainly will not sit back and play passive defense. They will counterattack. We don't know how well the Kodak printers will actually work at the end of the day. But that is not the point. The point is that Perez made the best move he possibly could. It deserves that exclamation point, even if Kodak eventually goes the way of Polaroid.

Before we move on, let's reemphasize something: It's called an *exchange sacrifice,* not an "exchange have-your-cake-and-eat-it-too." To pull these off, you have to really commit to the new idea and let go of the old one. The past is the past. That's the sacrifice part.

Such changes require serious commitment, and that can take new management. The Kodak CEO now says, "We made a mistake trying to execute the new plan with the old team." Reflecting on the fact that 10 of his 16 top reports are new at the company, he says, "You've got to burn the boats." Similarly, AOL has jettisoned large chunks of management previously affiliated with the content and subscription side of the house. And when Andy Grove and Gordon Moore decided to jettison their DRAM business in favor of microchips, they enacted a symbolic change, walking "out through the revolving door of their headquarters, departing as managers of the old business, and re-entered as managers of the new."[2]

IBM provides another fine example. The company's keen understanding of how essential business computing would become was the basis of the greatest technology hardware company in history. Their products became so much the standard that "you can't get fired for buying IBM" was the way all information technology pros thought about their purchase decisions.

But then it fell victim to the chess axiom, "There's nothing as hard to win as a won game." The hardware sales model was so ingrained in the company's culture that it made one of the greatest mistakes in modern business history by letting Microsoft, then a start-up, own the operating system (OS) on its new personal computer line. It simply never dawned on IBM that the OS could become the key value driver of a computer. (When it finally did wake up and created its own system, OS 2, it was too late and an enormous flop.)

As value moved from hardware to software, the great IBM got stuck in a classic commoditization trap. Nimzowitsch would smile knowingly and point out that although it did occupy a market space, it failed to overprotect it (surely he would have demanded owning the OS as well) and so suffered the predictable consequences.

How did Lou Gerstner turn this around? With an exchange sac. He gave up on standardized hardware products as the core of the company's business and leveraged the company's expertise and relationships in a new way, into a consulting and support practice. As part of the sacrifice, the company jettisoned the printer business and then the prestigious "Thinkpad" laptops, moves that would previously have been unthinkable. Today the business is about as far as imaginable from the classic days of everybody reporting to headquarters wearing the IBM uniform and selling the standard hardware product line. Indeed, fully one third of

IBM's employees no longer even report to a central office; instead, they're out in the field, working with the customers.

Meantime, its competitors are now trying to catch up, adding all sorts of additional services to their products. But it's awfully tough for anybody, even Microsoft or HP, to crack those big company relationships now, despite massive expenditures and reorganizations designed to do just that.

And, as it should, the sac has led to new lines of business not clearly seen when it was played. Even though IBM's main revenue source is now from services, its current hot growth engine is from software. Indeed, on a stand-alone basis, IBM's software unit would rank as the number 2 provider in the world, just after Microsoft; although it accounts for just 20 percent of revenue, it generates almost 40 percent of company earnings. That is pretty interesting, but the thing to focus on is how it arose: from customer relations and its enterprising sales force out there selling consulting services.

Steve Mills, head of the software unit, saw that the force had tremendous relationships but was underutilized. So he began a disciplined, low-risk acquisition strategy with a simple goal in mind: Purchase software companies whose major deficiency was breadth and depth of a sales force, thereby jump-starting the division's revenues. Sure enough, the approach has worked perfectly (essentially, as it also had earlier at Computer Associates). Of course, there's more to it than just the idea, and certainly Mills has done a fantastic job of integrating the targets into IBM and then integrating the products into his sales process. But the key to the success was seeing the new possibilities unleashed through the exchange sac.

Given that change is happening so rapidly, it's not surprising that some companies have to play exchange sacrifices early, and even often, in the game. This book started with how my little start-up had to do it, switching for a paid-for-license model to a free distribution model to get critical market mass through a deal with Microsoft. Another company that's had to be nimble with its business model early in its young life is Netflix.

This is the company, of course, that pioneered the non-video-store movie rental business. The core of the model was an amazing distribution network that provided mail delivery of any title within a day or two. And that was the basis of a large business. But as usual, others copied it, and their edge slipped away a bit. In particular, their old nemesis, Blockbuster, attacked with a combination of a physical store network and replicating the Netflix through-the-mail system. Even though it has never matched Netflix's mail delivery system, the idea of renting and returning through either route proved attractive, as did lower prices. The Netflix imbalance began slipping away.

So what did Netflix do? Smartly, it reconsidered its business model and played an exchange sacrifice, giving up reliance on its tremendous physical distribution advantage in favor of Internet delivery. (Of course, it really had no choice in the long run. The good move was seeing the trend, being realistic about it, and playing the sac early enough.) While others dawdled on this approach, worried about copy protection for Internet distribution, Netflix moved. The brilliant side of its concept was that, instead of allowing customers to download a movie (so that a whole copy was kept locally, ready to be ripped off), Netflix would "stream it." That way, because the whole thing never resides on the user's computer at one time, it can't be copied and redistributed.

More important, though, Netflix figured out a much better business model: charging by time spent watching movies, not by the number of movies chosen. That meant, among other things, that people could watch movies as they do TV and "change the channel" if it turned out that that early Jack Nicholson effort had remained unknown for a reason. Suddenly, most of the impediments to renting and watching movies vanished, just like the late fees had in version 1.0 of the business.

No doubt, such experiments will put the current income streams at risk. No doubt, that is absolutely essential. Nice move.

How Will the Network Execs Play It?

Speaking of entertainment, the television networks are now facing a full-blown crisis, the same one that previously disrupted the music industry. Their content is being reproduced and distributed for playback anytime, anywhere, in a fashion that strips out the traditional business model. The music world waited far too long to play its exchange sac and now is fighting to save an ugly endgame. Will the network execs play theirs in time?

Now, traditional broadcasters will not become irrelevant immediately; it's going to take a good while before bandwidth and processors get to be robust enough to handle routing all entertainment media over the Internet. But as night follows day, that will happen soon enough. The good news is that the networks do provide a valuable service: funding, developing, and selecting shows for our entertainment. They are important creators and filters (God forbid that the only videos out there are from YouTube freelancers!). They have powerful entertainment brands. The trick is to not be afraid of exchanging their current distribution advantage into other ways of preserving their brand and generating revenues.

The threat is quite real, of course, and illustrated well by two guys who are already featured in "Wanted Dead or Alive" posters hanging in Music and Telephony executive suites everywhere: Niklas Zennström and Janus Friis, the guys behind Kaaza (the music file-sharing program) and Skype (the free VOIP service). Their newest enterprise is Joost.

Joost is based on a novel insight about the way people want to consume video content on computers. Instead of chasing the idea that people would want to click around in interactive video spots just because computers let them do that, or aggregating two-bit content produced by bored college students, they had an epiphany: People, they figured, actually wanted to watch TV! They just don't want to worry about when a show is (or was) on the air.

So Joost is just TV over the Internet—from the users' point of view, that is. From an advertiser's point of view, it offers something much better than the over-the-air model: specific targeting of which ads are shown to which kinds of people and the ability to know exactly how many times a commercial was seen.

So let's think about this: The Internet TV model is better for the viewers and the advertisers and only worse for the networks. And the only current restraint on this model is the temporarily inadequate technology infrastructure. So, what do *you* think is going to happen long term?

The good news is that the TV guys watched the game the music execs were playing at the next table and have resolved not to make the same mistake. They're playing an exchange sac right now.

All the networks now provide at least some episodes free over the Web, after the original broadcast date, and the trend looks very likely to grow. This will indeed cannibalize some of their normal advertising revenue, as advertisers will pay less for sponsoring over-the-air shows with fewer viewers. And it is not clear how much this will be offset by the ad revenues generated by web distribution.

There's plenty of upside to playing this sac here and now. The networks can overcome their own bottlenecks in distribution of their valuable content by making their entire libraries of shows available for display and monetization at all times. Although they may never replace the sheer number of viewers they used to reach, one, they can charge more per ad view because of the targeting, and two, there's not a damn thing they can do about that, anyway. And the second point tells you that it is time to play the exchange sac right now, risk some traditional ad reviews, and get on with the new opportunity sets. If this particular idea doesn't work out, others might: For example, one can imagine a model under which customers "subscribe" to CBS and thus can retrieve any content in their library anytime, anywhere, on any device, commercial-free. Regardless, what they *cannot* do is pause, to "leave their finger on it," as we talked about in Chapter 4 ("On the Clock"), just because they are afraid of cannibalizing their traditional revenue source.

What this also illustrates is that it's the satellite and cable companies that have the most to fear, for they control precious little content . . . they are "only" a distribution play. Now, you might think, "Fine, but they can still be the providers of broadband access, so they're OK."

Fair enough, but the cable company business model is still deeply threatened. As discussed in Chapter 7, "Strong Squares," the Internet has driven a ruthless trend to efficient consumption, which is why album sales are so much farther down than are sales of singles. The analogy holds for cable TV: Why pay high monthly fees to get a huge number of shows you don't care about? The bet here is that consumers will begin to buy only what they want to watch and will initiate this shift by ordering programs à la carte via the Internet. The content owners can still make out fine this way; pure distributors will have a tougher time.

 ## LESSONS

1. If you begin to lose your imbalance, think about an exchange sac.
2. Look deeply into your products and service, intellectual property, and customer bases for new ideas that will drive the next phase of the business. Remember to separate what you're good at doing from the method of delivery; these days, a change there may be the key element of the sacrifice.
3. Play the sac before your advantage has wasted too far away. It's a conversion of an existing strength, so the longer you wait, the less you'll get back for it.
4. Commit! It's not called an "exchange have-your-cake-and-eat-it-too."
5. To get the organization to buy into a different business model, management changes may be necessary. Everyone's got to be a believer.

CHAPTER NINE

CLASSIC
TACTICS

Needless to say, the millions of chess games played over the years have involved more kinds of clever ideas and beautiful combinations than we've talked about so far or, indeed, that could ever be captured in one book. Nonetheless, a few classics appear over and over again and, having read this far, you'll be able to guess that we see several of them as nice business blueprints.

Of course, any good player must both attack and defend. So one thing we'll see here is how some of the most successful companies of the past 30 years, like Microsoft and Wal-Mart, have deployed chess ideas both to expand their markets and to protect them. As we progress, we'll also see another key point: that the best offensive strategies also provide defensive benefits, and vice versa. The very best moves of all are those that achieve both sets of aims at one go.

PRINCIPLES OF ATTACK

The most important single principle of attack is this: "The target cannot be chosen at will; the attack must be directed at the weak points in the enemy position".[1] Attacking a well-protected area just because it happens to be directly in front of you is dumb.

As obvious as this may seem, businesses frequently launch new attacks against enemy strong points. They like to just do what they're already comfortable doing, regardless of what the actual situation is in the area they're trying to invade. That results from focus on core competencies rather than imbalances. Your company may be very good at something, but that still doesn't mean that you can simply outcompete an entrenched opponent. You've got to find places where exploiting that capability will yield breakthroughs.

Marks & Spencer is a world-class company. It has a centuries-old reputation for quality and a deep knowledge of supply-chain management and its British consumers. But it has had enormous difficulties in transporting its success from the British Isles for a simple reason: What it is good at over there doesn't hit at a weak point over here. It has spent years attacking strong points of entrenched competitors, with little to show for all the effort.

In chess, a famous weak spot is f7. That's because at the beginning of the game, it is only defended by the king; a lot of gambit openings, therefore, try to create quick attacks against this square. But in many developed positions, and in most businesses, one of the most tempting weak spots to attack is the base of a pawn chain.

TARGET THE BASE OF A PAWN CHAIN

Pawn chains are monsters to face. They control giant chunks of board territory and shut down the operation of your big pieces; they can suffocate you. And there's a big problem trying to break them down. Because of the way pawns capture, if you do grab one of these guys, another just takes its place in the line. It's a little like Hercules and the Hydra: Cut off one head, and another springs up in its place.

It can look much the same when surveying a market controlled by a major company. It has so much size, so many existing customers, that we've got no space to operate in. We can't launch an all-out attack on the broad market; it has the resources, credibility, and relationships to crush us.

So, what should you do? Attack the *base* of the chain.

Check this diagram. See how the White pawns form a "chain" running from b2 to e5? Now, note that the guy on b2 is the only

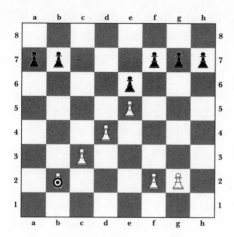

THE RIGHT WAY TO ATTACK AN
ESTABLISHED COMPETITOR:
AT THE BASE OF HIS VALUE CHAIN

one not protected by another pawn. That's where you have to start; then, you can work your way up to the pawn on c3, then d4, and only then e5.

And so it goes in business. Generally, successful companies have a product that is bought by different types of customers, and these companies naturally pay the most attention to the customers providing the greatest profit margins, the top of their "chain." You'll rarely be successful in attacking that head pawn, the one furthest into high-value customer territory with a tremendous amount of organizational support behind it. Instead, you need to look down and attack at the "base of the chain" with specialized products at the lower end of the price spectrum.

This can be particularly effective with technology that has the chance to improve rapidly. The new technology or product gets established with some customers for whom a lower-priced, lower-functioning product is good enough (customers who the established company does not care much about), and then it works its way up the chain as the technology improves. This is exactly how Sony gained access to the U.S. electronics market.

What Sony understood better than anybody in consumer electronics was the importance of the transistor as the change agent that would make consumer electronics take off. This hallmark invention of the twentieth century was born in the all-American institution Bell Laboratories, but it was a little company halfway around the world that saw how it could be used to collapse the pawn chains of the masters of the electronics world.

In the early 1950s, televisions and radios were housed in big, living-room-sized units with tremendous sound quality, wonderful craftsmanship, and vacuum-tube hearts. RCA and GE looked at the lowly transistor and scoffed: The tinny sound that miniature radios could produce would never be a threat to the high-profit, big-dollar units at the top of their chains.

Sony's Akio Morita, then a junior executive on the move up, had a different view. He came to the United States to license the right to use transistors in radios. Showing just how much of a surprise the upcoming attack was going to be, Western Electric, the Bell System's manufacturing arm, took an unimaginably paltry $25,000 in return.

Soon thereafter, Sony produced its first portable radio, which weighed 20 percent as much as a vacuum-tube radio, cost two-thirds less, and sported a clean, stylish design—a hallmark of Sony products to this day. Sony quickly geared up for mass production, eclipsing a small U.S. radio manufacturer, Regency, that actually had brought out the first transistorized portable radio on the U.S. market. As GE and RCA accurately predicted, the sound quality of Sony's tiny radios wasn't there. But so what? You could take one anywhere, and they were cheap. It was, indeed, no substitute for that wonderful family radio in the living room, but for junior to listen to the ball game while out with friends, it was just fine.

Within a handful of years, portable radios became extremely popular, and Sony had completely captured the base of the radio pawn chain. Then, as the quality of the new technology improved, Sony used its inherently cheaper manufacturing costs to move up the chain, eventually conquering the entire industry. As is frequently the case, once the base goes, it's difficult to stop the attack: The established competitors were locked in to higher-priced methods and parts and were relatively helpless.

A nearly identical attack caused Xerox to lose its viselike grip on the copier market. As GE and RCA had, Xerox focused its attention on the powerful "head" pawns, its big office customers. Those customers provided a huge percentage of the companies' profits, after all, so concentrating its service and sales efforts there was completely logical. This strategy maximizes returns on capital in the short term, but, of course, we know what happens when that base pawn falls.

Like Sony's radio exploit, Canon did not try to offer a copier with all the bells and whistles that Xerox offered, nor did it pretend to have the same speed or quality. What it did do was go after just the base pawn to start. Canon attacked specific functions in small offices (those of doctors and dentists, for example) with limited-function, simple-to-operate, and much-lower-priced machines. These cheap copiers supplied everything the base of the pawn chain needed, and Xerox couldn't afford to spend the resources to defend the square. As is nearly always the case, they were too busy worrying about the top of the chain. But once Canon got the first pawn, it started working its way up.

These days, this same sort of battle is being fought in the automotive sector. For all the laurels being cast on Toyota and Honda, the ex-base pawn attackers, there are some impressive new players who've also learned the trick.

Ever heard of Tata Motors? You will. It's India's leading car manufacturer, and it's got its sights set on a vehicle that will retail for something like $2,500. Of course, it will lack key features that Americans consider essential, like antilock brakes and airbags, and may not pass American air-quality standards. So it'll be easy for the big boys to write it off, just as RCA and Xerox did with their attackers. But in making a $2,500 car, Tata is picking up enormous experience in how to cut costs to the bone, both in the materials (for every single part and subpart) and the manufacturing process itself. It will undoubtedly gain crucial know-how that the bigger companies lack, and when it begins its march up the pawn chain, everybody had better watch out. It might seem laughable to think that Toyota or Honda could ever wind up like General Motors, but if they leave that base pawn unprotected, they'll be sitting in the automotive old folks' home right beside Grandma herself.

It's not just manufactured goods that are subject to this sort of attack. The reason that AOL lost its preeminent position was that bare-bones ISPs, which were not offering anything remotely similar to AOL's rich content, e-mail addresses, and instant-messaging services, did offer to get you on the Internet at a fraction of the cost. AOL was excruciatingly slow to respond to this attack on its base, preferring to nurture its high-margin head pawns for so long that, ultimately, it had to play the exchange sac described in the previous chapter and toss its entire business model.

Similar things are afoot even in health care. Sure, we all want a great doctor when we've got a serious problem. But do I really have to wait days for an appointment, and then a couple of hours in the office, just to get more of that pink stuff for my kid's third ear infection this year? That's the base of the medical industry's pawn chain: the common, standard, boring, everyday illnesses.

Finally, this base pawn is under attack. A host of retail medical clinics are sprouting up in pharmacies and retailers like Wal-Mart, promising quick, inexpensive treatment for routine illnesses and injuries. Interestingly, firms like Redi-Clinic and Minute-Clinic (its slogan: "When You're Sick, We're Quick"), among the fastest growing, have also taken the "pawn base" strategy the farthest: They use nurse-practitioners instead of physicians for much of their care. Like European pharmacies, these clinics are faster and cheaper sources of routine care than are doctors' offices and good enough for a big percentage of medical needs. According to chess theory, their plan is going to work just fine.

THE MINORITY ATTACK

Often the enemy has no apparent weakness. Time to create one!

There's an intriguing *Rocky* sequel shaping up in the tech world, a grudge match, in which IBM seeks to reclaim its crown as champion of office computing from the upstart who took it away, Microsoft. And it shows that maybe IBM really did learn something from those Deep Blue vs. Kasparov matches, for it's basing its challenge on a classic chess tactic, the minority attack.

The chess idea works like this. Let's say all the hot action in a game is over on the Kingside. Suddenly, one of the players, who has only two pawns on the Queenside, launches them toward a group of three enemy Queenside pawns. Since two can't beat three, why would he do that? Because if they're exchanged one for one, the opponent will be left with a lone pawn far away from the main action. That will tough to defend, and when resources are diverted from the Kingside to protect it, the first player will have an easier time attacking in the area of the board he's really interested in.

And that's what IBM is doing to Microsoft as it launches a free product called Symphony, a suite of word processing, spreadsheet, and collaboration software. Interestingly, it's based on the same open-source code as similar products from Sun and Google, indirectly giving those products a push at the same time.

Can any of this freeware outgun Office? In a word, no. Microsoft has over 500 million Office users and is selling over 70 million licenses a year for the software. Business users' needs for assured compatibility, security, and instant familiarity make that installed base look like an insurmountable advantage, certainly in the medium term. IBM knows that full well, but it's got a plan.

By undertaking an attack on this side of the board—and supporting the same platform that Sun and Google are using—IBM is forcing Microsoft to divert focus and resources away from what IBM sees as the main battleground: selling other enterprise software into corporate America, like its Websphere suite. To the extent that contact, e-mail, and spreadsheet software become free, corporate budgets to buy other software will increase. That's the side of the board IBM really cares about.

THE RULE OF TWO WEAKNESSES

We know that we want to find, or even create, a weak spot to attack. But even when clear targets are present, the best players can stage tenacious and successful defenses. However, once the defender has committed all his resources to shoring up one area, attacking another will often yield the critical breakthrough. Players call this phenomenon the "rule of two weaknesses."

Such attacks can be effective in the business world as well. Think about one of the more interesting one-on-one matches in modern business: Intel versus AMD (formerly Advanced Micro Devices, Inc.). For a long time, Intel ignored its upstart competitor and assumed that a one-dimensional attack strictly based on superior technology would win the day. This did work for a while, but in 2003 AMD showed up with a chip, called the Opteron, aimed at the relatively narrow but lucrative market segment for corporate servers. AMD finally had a clear performance lead in a space in which Intel did not have a new chip coming out immediately. The major manufacturers for the first time took AMD seriously enough to include its chip in their products. Within a few years, AMD's share of this market zoomed to over 20 percent.

Intel counterattacked and, three years after the Opteron hit the market, was finally able to deliver a real one-up of its own: the Clovertown, which packs four computing cores onto a single chip and has proved an effective response. On a more profound level, just as the natural limits of silicon chips were being reached, it also invented a new material combination that promises to allow it to continue to produce ever-faster processors. But AMD defended with the Athlon, based on its own new alloy. Try as it might, Intel couldn't crack AMD with an all-out R&D attack.

So it employed the rule of the two weaknesses. Just as AMD poured new money into R&D, Intel dramatically dropped its prices, attacking an entirely different point. AMD doesn't have the resources to match that pricing and keep up its new development efforts. It has to make a choice about what to defend and, for now, AMD seems to be in trouble. In 2007, it lost half of its market value. It's a good player, and we know it'll respond; but Intel's two-pronged attack has certainly been effective as of this writing.

The battle of the "V"s, Verizon versus Vonage, is another example. Vonage was the early leader in the paid voice-over-Internet protocol (VOIP) market. It got off to a fast start with big venture capital backing and then obtained a nice cash war chest with an IPO. It was gaining customers quickly, cutting into Verizon's profitable landline user base.

Much to its credit, instead of worrying about possible cannibalization of its landline business, Verizon initially responded by bringing a matching VOIP service to market. But Vonage was scrappy, and it held its own with a massive marketing campaign; it even fought off Verizon's ferocious legal attack. In addition, it added 166,000 sub-scribers in the first quarter of 2007, even at the cost of a $73 million loss. It was putting up a tenacious defense to Verizon's attack.

Verizon then launched a second thrust, one that Vonage could not simultaneously defend: It bundled the VOIP service with cable TV delivery and Internet access into a single well-priced package. Verizon not only reversed the tide of rapidly increasing new VOIP customer sign-ups by Vonage but is now winning that battle outright.

There is a point of particular interest here. Verizon could have tried to defend its franchise without offering VOIP services; its actual strategy meant losing money that it may have been able to extract from its own customers by keeping them on traditional wired service longer. But that would have been a one-dimensional attack that would have permitted Vonage to press its advantage in VOIP. By first attacking with its own service and then bundling it with functions Vonage couldn't match, Verizon overwhelmed its opponent and effectively ended the game before too much dam-age to its customer base occurred.

OPEN UP

Chess strategies can often be categorized as *open* or *closed*. Although it is sometimes safer and easier to play a closed system early in the game, continuing the pattern for too long usually spells trouble. In the business world, that exact dynamic often provides attacking chances for companies willing to play an open system.

What is an open system? In the chess world, it refers to a cer-tain style of freewheeling, fluid play, one that involves more pieces in the action; it is more interactive, less prescribed. It is a system that mixes it up, rather than hunkering down inside a well-dug foxhole.

Closed systems keep more control. They seek a certain, strict setup of the pieces. They are more inwardly focused, refusing to take much account of the way the world is reacting. They are a "build-your-fort" approach, an old-school seize-your-market-territory-and-keep-it philosophy.

In chess, closed systems work best in the early stages of the game, and they work best in business in the early stages of an industry. Indeed, they can be necessary when the goal is to create a major behavioral shift. That's because for big changes to be successful, several new and different pieces must be codeveloped to assure interoperability. Apple loves closed systems for that reason. The iPod was a phenomenon because of a beautiful integration of several new pieces: a unique device, yes, but also a business-model-busting library of songs and elegant software to tie everything together. All the components had to be codeveloped for the system to function well.

But over time, as the solutions that closed systems provide become standardized, the need for the whole system to be closed diminishes. That's when the benefits of open systems become overwhelming. Remember, even the iPod became a runaway hit only when its associated software was produced for Windows machines and no longer required buying a Mac.

The ultimate example of the power of an open system to crack a closed one is how Microsoft cored Apple in the "first world war" for the PC market, fought in the late eighties and early nineties. You'll remember that at the beginning, Windows and Mac machines had relatively similar market shares. But Microsoft opened up: It provided all software developers with hooks into the operating system (OS) that allowed third parties to write applications for Windows machines.

Apple decided to stay closed, both business-model-wise and physically (it actually took special tools just to open the original Macs for customization or repair). But more important, Apple carefully limited who could write applications for its system. This assured that its beautiful, seamless, user experience would be guarded and also that it'd have a big piece of all associated revenues.

The problem for Apple was that Microsoft's open game introduced far more pieces into the action than Apple's could: Outside developers saw they could make money by writing and selling applications for Windows, so they did. That flooded the stores with software for Windows, which made those machines fundamentally more useful to consumers, so many more people bought them. Once this dynamic started to work, Apple couldn't control it, and the cycle spun into total domination by Microsoft.

But what about the fact that being open in this way gives away so much economic value to outside developers? Well, although the company playing the open system does not get all the benefit of it, so much total value is created that capturing just a good piece of it is far better than capturing all the incremental value that is accreting inside a closed system.

The strategy has been brushed off and put into action by Facebook as it attacks MySpace. As of this writing, Facebook was only about a third as large as MySpace, but it has now opened up. It says it wants to be the "operating system of social networks" and is thus making available so-called APIs, software hooks into its system so that anyone can write programs that will integrate with the site and, just as in the Microsoft example, take whatever money can be generated from them. (Interestingly, it was a very crude and accidental version of this idea that helped make MySpace so popular to begin with: Because people could simply write HTML code into MySpace pages, they were capable of adding interesting items to their pages. But this approach was far too crude for mass adoption.)

Within days of the publication of the APIs, thousands of Web 2.0 developers were racing to leverage the MySpace user base for their own purposes. For example, several developers are sprinting to be the main music-sharing software of Facebook, and bring it to or beyond parity with the analogous MySpace service. Seeing what's coming, MySpace has now responded in kind. It's teamed up with Google and many of its own smaller competitors to create a "universal" set of standards for writing programs that plug into social network sites, in an initiative called "Open Social." They hope to be able to attract the legions of developers to this platform because, in principle, applications that work on one social site will work on all. So, for MySpace and Facebook, it's truely "open" warfare.

Even Sun Microsystems has become a believer. One of the early stars of high-end computing, it aggressively pursued a closed-system approach in its early life; indeed, its founder and CEO was fond of doing battle with his perceived opponents, especially the "Wintel duopoly." Sun's high-end systems used only their own chips and own OS, Solaris. Although the company did well for a while, as commodity computers became more and more capable of handling previously high-end tasks, the company ran into serious problems. After five successive years of losses, even the famously combative Sun began to realize that it could not sustain its closed posture, regardless of how many rounds of layoffs it underwent.

Things began to change after Jonathan Schwartz took over as CEO. He went on the attack by opening up the OS to developers, customers, and other hardware providers. Of course, the main idea is to get the development community to drive further use of Solaris by creating programs that run on it, taking a page out of Microsoft's "Competitive Operating Systems 101" playbook. An equally important advantage of the approach is that it removes customers' biggest fear: that the closed-system provider will go out of business and leave it reliant on a system without support or future development. This has allowed it to be more successful with ultrahigh-end customers who need advanced systems but cannot risk being stuck if Sun sets. Opening up turned things around just in time.

Perhaps the greatest-ever test of the open system philosophy is now upon us. Can Google's gPhone unseat the Windows Mobile and Symbian platforms and perhaps even the iPhone? Google's plan is to give away a new, completely open software platform to handset makers and let outside parties develop to it, so that it will rapidly gain new features. The logic is simple: Because it's free, smartphone makers will want to use it. But Google will make sure it can serve ads into the platform, so it'll make money in its usual way.

Very smart. Will it work? Maybe not. The wrinkle is that there are zillions of peculiar little issues involved in telephony that can vary by handset configuration and carrier standards. Developing software of that sort is something Google has never done, but at which Microsoft and Nokia are experts. And perhaps more importantly, bad guys can write to open systems just as easily as good guys can. Because security is just a touch more important for office phone calls and e-mail than it is for the "I'm fluent in sarcasm" Facebook group, an open platform might not be your CTO's first choice for the office smartphone standard.

Moreover, in attempting to compete with the iPhone, Google is taking on a powerful integrated combination of software and hardware; it's hard to compete with only half the equation. Apple's ability to iterate on both sides simultaneously should provide a continuing edge over Google, just as it should over Microsoft. Finally, although Google's threat to push the gPhone along by purchasing spectrum is interesting, here's the key question: If they do, who's actually going to run the network? Like designing the underlying software itself, doing that requires a lot of specialized expertise. As Roger Entner of IAG Research says, "An open system is really awesome if you don't have to operate it."[2]

Exactly: even open systems need players to play them. *Completely* open movements usually fail because there is no one to reset the overall direction at major turning points. That's why the open-source Linux movement is unlikely to ultimately unseat Windows. And while the success of the open-source Firefox browser is certainly impressive, it's hard to ignore its Netscape roots or its heavy Google financing as key reasons that it has captured so much of the market.

Anyway, this is a business book, and we disapprove of anticapitalist motives! Our lesson is that smart companies can leverage the abilities (and, yes, the greed) of the entire outside world in the attack on a competitor, and that's a pretty powerful set of pieces to bring into the game.

PRINCIPLES OF DEFENSE

Historically, companies could rely on a slew of entrenchment techniques to protect themselves. Big plants, skilled workforces, favorable raw materials contracts, better distribution channels—all were fairly effective, at least against smaller competitors. But no longer. The information revolution and globalization have made these defensive stalwarts into dry moats.

Most recently, the deterrent of choice became "business process" patents, of which a trickle turned into a flood. But a judicial and legislative backlash against this trend has become evident, and rightly so: Should Amazon.com really be able to block BarnesandNoble.com from selling books online with a single click because they patented that "invention?" Or should Netflix stop Blockbuster from delivering movies by mail? Whatever happens on the legal front with such patents, they are rarely genuinely effective in any event.

Once really smart people see something novel, they can almost always reverse-engineer it in a way that avoids blatant patent infringement. (As one software genius I know says, "The important thing is to know that something *can* be done. After that, it's always possible to find several ways to do it.") Once the infringement is less than blatant, the patent is not so effective. For every Blackberry and Vonage situation, in which there were meaningful threats to shut down a business, there are zillions of cases where a flurry of cease-and-desist letters yields either nothing at all or at best a modest settlement. As a real method of protecting your business, forget it.

Instead, you want to play like "Sweet Pea," one of the regular blitz chess players in the corner of Washington Square Park. He nearly always wins, although he doesn't know too much about defense. Instead, he plays rapid, high-pressure offense and spews a lot of good trash talk. Maybe you won't get to shout "Hey, baby, where's that Bishop gonna go?" very often. But the basic style is correct: Pressure works.

One of the great chess writers, in his own restrained early-twentieth-century style, put it this way, "It is a typical beginner's mistake to go on the defensive at the first sign of attack: guarding against non-existent dangers can involve giving up all possibilities of active counter-play."[3] That is, you've got to keep pushing your ideas even when you see threats on the horizon. Just as directing an attack at a weak spot is the most important offensive idea, the most important defensive idea is that the best defense really is a good offense. And good offenses are built on speed.

OFFENSE AS DEFENSE: RAPID ITERATION

Over the past 20 years, no company has played pressure defense better than Microsoft. Its policy of rapidly incorporating new trends into its products, instead of trying to maintain the status quo, is the "Sweet Pea" model of offense as defense. Microsoft's own somewhat Orwellian name for it is "embrace and extend."

The story of how Microsoft got started is the stuff of legend. In 1981, IBM needed an operating system to run its new line of personal computers. Negotiations with the leading OS company of the day, Digital Research, weren't going well, and Bill Gates was able to intercede and win the business with a "Disk Operating System," DOS, that he'd just bought from another company for $75,000. That princely sum was to be the foundation of one of the great fortunes in history.

IBM agreed to use the system, but instead of getting an exclusive or buying the code outright, it let Microsoft keep the rights to license the OS to end users and other manufacturers. After all, who cared about selling software? The money was in the hardware. (A really dreadful chess mistake is known as a "blunder." If there ever was a business move that qualified for the description, this was it.)

We've already noted how Microsoft's "open" approach won the early PC wars. Now what we want to see is how the company has responded to the many profound challenges it has faced over the years as the computing world has undergone one metamorphosis after another.

You might date yourself by remembering what a "DOS Command Line" was. In the early days, my children, there were no such things as graphical user interfaces (GUIs), point and click, or even a "mouse." As recounted earlier, all were more or less invented at Xerox Research Park and then popularized by Apple in 1984. This breakthrough in how humans interacted with computers was an early and major test for the boys from Redmond, Washington. Make no mistake about who the "Big Brother" was supposed to be in that classic ad that introduced the Mac.

The response was the first use of embrace and extend (unless you count the fact that Gates actually bought DOS from another company in the nick of time—he sure embraced and extended that operating system!). Instead of trying to defend its basic user interface, Microsoft quickly switched to one it saw as better: "Windows" extended the DOS system by creating window panes on your screen. Critics rightly charged that building a GUI on top of DOS like this yielded a clumsy result, but so what? For the first of many times, the company defended its position successfully by instantly incorporating a new trend, rather than resisting it.

This approach was refined over the next several years. Would-be competitors would no sooner invent new kinds of software functionality than they would find the idea incorporated for free in the next iteration of Windows: disk-maintenance utilities; compression methods; audio, picture, and video playback; and advanced game play features were all embraced and extended as part of the OS. Then the same started to happen with content: Titles like Encarta, Money, and Aviator showed just how suffocating that Microsoft embrace could be.

The company cruised along this way for years. But in the late nineties, a profoundly new challenge emerged as the Internet caught hold. Now, just adding new functions to desktop software was no longer enough.

After briefly hiding its head in the sand about this tectonic shift in computing, Microsoft was awakened by a famous Bill Gates call-to-arms memo. And the troops responded: Instead of trying harder and harder to wed users to their desktops rather than their Web connections, it reversed course and charged. Internet Explorer not only caught Netscape Navigator, it effectively eliminated it; now, Internet Explorer accounts for something like 90 percent of all browsers. The thrust also resulted in the creation of a major business unit, MSN, that now generates something like $2 billion in annual ad revenues (prior to seeing returns from its purchase of advertising firm Aquantive). Rapid iteration sure beats the heck out of passive defense.

Again: For a while around 2000, it began to look as though video game terminals could turn into the family computing hub. After all, it's where the next generation was spending its time; the machines really were powerful little computers; and as online game play became more common, they were being used to connect through the Web as well. Everyone was beginning to talk convergence while eyeing that Playstation under the TV.

This would have been an easy trend to ignore for a "serious" computing company. But to Microsoft's credit, it continued to play true to its style, to embrace video game consoles as a potentially important rival to the PC and extend their functionality. It fused its fantastic knowledge of computer graphics to a unit with the best visuals on the market but, as important given its long-term concerns, emphasized a robust system for allowing players in disparate locations to compete against each other through the Internet.

After several years of losses that had analysts howling, the strategy has started to work, and the Xbox has indeed given the company a toehold in the convergence door. Its Xbox LIVE marketplace, an adjunct to the system for networked play, has suddenly become a rapidly growing distribution channel for movies and other entertainment content. Best of all, the users represent a healthy percentage of that young male audience that's gone missing from the Nielsen ratings. Note that the massive investment in Xbox still has not paid off in dollars and cents, but it certainly has provided a strong defense through offense from an attack on its home computing franchise.

The company is now facing two new and very interesting challenges. One of these sounds like something out of *The Matrix:* "virtual machines." This is software that resides between the computer hardware and the traditional operating system and thus allows the computer to run more than one OS; for example, it permits the same physical machine to operate Windows and Linux. But because of where it resides in the system, it also permits one Windows license to be effectively operated by a network of physical computers, thereby undercutting the basic Microsoft business model.

The leading company in this field is VMware, currently growing at something like 100 percent year over year, and it's closing in on $2 billion of annual revenue. Those are real numbers, but for Microsoft, the much more important issue is the strategic threat: The company that controls the layer of software closest to the hardware is the one that really controls how the machine behaves. That's Microsoft's strong square, and you can bet it isn't going to play passive defense in the face of this challenge.

The second major challenge is the minority attack discussed above, the IBM- and Google-led Web services assault. If it works, certainly this is just as fundamental a challenge as virtual machines. So how will Microsoft respond?

You know: Embrace and extend. Just like everything from multimedia capabilities to compression software to Web browsers, these new functions will simply become integrated into future versions of Vista and the Office Suite. Rapid iteration, offense as defense, will once again be tested, and our guess is that it will once again be successful.

On the virtual machine side, the beauty of this approach, as it always has been, is that other developers of virtual machine software will work with Microsoft to make sure their products will be fully compatible with the dominant OS. Maybe their products will even get incorporated in some way and give them a distribution edge over VMware. But you can bet that Microsoft will put itself in control of the software, just as it did in the little story that started this book.

As to Web services: ditto. Microsoft will almost certainly begin to build into its OS features that will allow Web access (and modification) to any document, along with easy collaboration, and of course, it'll be able to offer free storage on its own servers. It'll offer 80 percent of the advantages others will, but with 100 percent certainty of reliability and interoperability with key desktop applications. So far, that's been enough, and it's likely to be again.

It is this counterattacking, rapid-iteration style that makes the company so prosperous through the utterly unpredictable technology tides and the regular appearance of unexpected threats.

Respond to Wing Attacks with One in the Center

When you start getting cornered in one part of the board, you can't let yourself get smothered; instead, generating counterplay in another part is essential. One of the most basic defensive ideas in chess is this: If attacked on a wing, counterpunch in the center.

A gorgeous example is Nintendo's fight back against the aforementioned Xbox and the Sony Playstation. The company (which, you may be surprised to hear, is actually over 100 years old and began as a maker of playing cards) had dominated the business in the '80s and early '90s. But it slipped to third place because it was unable to match the ever-improving graphics capabilities of the Playstation and Xbox that hard-core gamers craved.

Nintendo was in deep trouble. It simply did not have the raw technology horsepower of its two rivals; it could not defend the attack on the extreme end of the gaming market. So instead of just backpedaling against the oncoming assault, like a good chess player, Nintendo opened a new front in the middle of the board. Essentially ignoring the hard-core gamers and their graphics-hungry, hypercomplex fantasy worlds, Nintendo went after a broader middle market for simple, fun, multiplayer games.

It attacked in the center with a new model, the Wii. It included a key new feature, a motion-based game controller that allowed players to smack tennis balls and roll at bowling pins with big, sweeping motions of their arms that emulated real play. This wasn't a terribly amazing technology achievement; motion sensors themselves had been around a long time. But they had been ignored in the wing attacks for the serious gamers, which instead featured ultrarealistic 3D graphics and first-person shooter games. Suddenly, newspaper photos started showing old folks at a Wii "bowling tournament" right in the middle of a nursing home. It's hard to imagine the analogous shot, one of Great-Aunt Agatha playing "Final Fantasy."

The joke in the industry, in fact, became that we were in the middle of the "Wii-sixty revolution": People were starting to buy a

Wii to have fun with friends over and an Xbox 360 for intense, immersive one-player games.

Interestingly, another part of hitting back in the middle involved the developers themselves. The cost of programming new games for the super-sophisticated Xbox and Sony platforms had escalated to tens of millions of dollars, a huge gamble to take for most game development companies. Meantime, the price of creating a Nintendo game stayed in the low single digits of millions, a much easier nut to cover with modest sales.

In accordance with chess theory, this central counterattack has been wildly successful. The Wii began outselling the Playstation 3 by a huge margin, and fairly incredibly, Nintendo's market capitalization caught and passed Sony's just a few months after the product was released.

An analogous story is playing out now in the cell phone world. Palm essentially invented modern smartphones, and certainly was the industry thought leader throughout the '90s. But like a marathoner at twenty miles, it "hit the wall" at the turn of the century. Its operating system, once so innovative, became sluggish and buggy as compared to the Blackberry and Windows Mobile platforms, and it certainly lacks the vision or technology prowess to keep up with the iPhone. Very much like Nintendo, it suddenly found itself being outflanked by latecomers with substantially better technology resources and vision. It could no longer compete on that wing of the board.

So it counterattacked in the middle with the aptly named Centro, a cheaper and smaller version of its flagship Treo. Instead of trying to be ever more advanced in its feature set to compete for the high-end, fringe market, it turned back to the center and delivered the old feature set into the vast—and vulnerable—middle market. Let Apple and Microsoft duke it out over the relatively small number of users willing to pay $500 for a phone; Palm will instead sell lots of units to the $100 crowd, thanks very much.

The approach doesn't just work when competitors have gotten beyond you on the high end of the market, as was the case for Nintendo and Palm. You can see the same motif at work at the other extreme.

Target, for example, moved toward the center when Wal-Mart's attack on the low-price wing of the market became overwhelming. Wal-Mart's logistical and buying-size advantages were simply too much to overcome. So Target went back toward the center of the market by establishing a trendier identity and, importantly, moving into fashion. That last part is especially important because the skills necessary to buy, ship, and stock consumer staples is a far cry from the skill set necessary to understand and capitalize on fashion trends. Thus, Target sidestepped the brunt of Wal-Mart's attack, its ability to offer the lowest possible prices on staples, and struck back in the middle of the market.

A similar thing is happening to Wal-Mart's grocery business. For example, Publix cannot hope to match Wal-Mart's prices, so it has hit back in the middle with a superior experience for customers not totally desperate to save every nickel. Publix is the top supermarket for it, according to the American Consumer Satisfaction Index; Wal-Mart is last.

Chess theory says that the player who's committed to an all-out attack on a wing will have trouble responding to a central counterattack. That's because the offensive setup involved is inherently inflexible.

It's the same in business; Wal-Mart's wing strategy has impeded its ability to respond to the Target and Publix central counterattacks. Being way out on the price wing requires massive inventory standardization, but customers have localized tastes, and the middle market doesn't mind paying a bit more to satisfy them. For example, Publix offers the sweetened tea that southerners love, and pigs feet and red beans for the Hispanic crowd. National standardization just isn't going to work for those products. Proving the efficacy of this approach, Publix is showing same-store sales trends going north while Wal-Mart's go south. Even better, those sales are more profitable: Publix makes 40 percent more on grocery sales than Wal-Mart does.

This basic idea works across all industries. Look, for example, at how Charles Schwab, king of the discount brokers, returned from semiretirement to reposition his eponymous company. It floundered after his departure, reeling from declining trading in the early-2000's bear market and attacks by ultra-low-priced online brokers. Being a good player, he realized that his formerly successful strategy had petered out and that he could not outdiscount the new generation of online brokers out on the wing. So he moved the attack back to the middle of the board by refocusing his company on providing higher-margin services to high-net-worth individuals, many of them served by advisers who work with Schwab. The company has seen a nice recovery and remains king of the highly lucrative business-serving registered investment advisers catering to the wealthy.

PROPHYLAXIS

Another of Nimzowitsch's pet ideas was "prophylaxis." Here the idea is to cut off your opponent's opportunities to create threats before they materialize. Although most businesspeople automatically think this means patent protection, there are other and sometimes more effective ways to go about it.

Let's revisit Wal-Mart for a moment, for Sam Walton was one of the most successful prophylaxis players in business history. As noted in "Lucky or Good?" (Chapter 6), Wal-Mart's big idea early on was to move into markets that were just big enough to support a single large discounter and no bigger: A rival could not justify spending the money to open a second big box in Wal-Mart towns. That in turn meant that the company kept gaining buying power and logistical advantages, enabling it to move to ever-lower prices. Only after establishing a juggernaut did Wal-Mart attack larger markets.

This was a prime example of prophylaxis and one that shows again the benefit of integrating offensive and defensive moves: The manner in which Wal-Mart handled its expansion and garnered ever-increasing cost advantages also blocked its opponents from a counterattack. It was a marvel of modern business strategy.

Toys "R" Us pulled off a variation of the same idea—for a while—when the big warehouse discounters first started carrying toys. Faced with an internal study that showed the new warehouse clubs would grow quickly and that their foray into toys was working, Toys "R" Us came up with an interesting prophylaxis idea: force the toy manufacturers to choose between them (a huge reseller) and the new clubs (small but growing). They simply told the suppliers that if they sold to the warehouses, they'd lose Toys "R" Us as a customer. Nearly all agreed, staving off a major threat for a couple of years. Unfortunately, Toys "R" Us didn't use that time to build a more defensible model, and eventually the dike caved in.

On a smaller scale, Jet Blue deployed this sort of tactic by buying up the company that provided the technology for its popular satellite TV service, something that distinguished it from its competition. Similarly, it entered into a long-term contract to buy all the planes of a certain type that Embraer, the Brazilian jet manufacturer, could produce and that it thought were critical to profitability on certain routes. Both illustrate an excellent way to play the strategy: Lock up all the output of key industry providers.

No doubt my favorite example of this strategy was executed by Minnetonka's CEO Robert Taylor when he concocted the idea for Softsoap, the first popular liquid hand soap. Faced with a great idea that couldn't be patented and massive competitors who could knock the idea off in a second and easily outmarket and outdistribute Minnetonka, Taylor reached deep into the Nimzowitsch playbook.

How? He recognized that the big trick of making the product successful was its hand-pump dispenser, and no matter how big P&G was, it didn't make or have those. So he bought all the capacity of the only two hand-pump suppliers by placing an order for 100 million of them, at a cost that exceeded Minnetonka's net worth. When Softsoap was a hit, the potential competitors couldn't move; there were simply no hand pumps to buy. This gorgeous maneuver gave Softsoap a year-and-a-half lead in the market, during which it established a brand that consumers loved and that kept it successful long after the big boys finally found some pumps.

♞ LESSONS

1. The best moves integrate offensive and defensive characteristics, rather than treating them as separate subjects.
2. The biggest rule of attack is to locate the weakest target, not the most convenient one; core competencies alone are usually inadequate to beat strong, entrenched competitors.

   A typical weak spot is the base of a pawn chain, the lowest end of the competitors' product-customer set. If the opponent doesn't have any obvious weaknesses, think about trying a "minority attack": Launch a disruptive business model against one of its key products to divert resources from your real target.
3. Leverage resources outside your company for your attack by playing an open game.
4. The best defense is a good offense; counterplay, usually through rapid product iteration, is crucial to stave off attacks. Specifically, if a competitor has achieved an overwhelming advantage on one edge of a market, counterpunch in the middle.
5. Prophylaxis, the art of shutting down an attack before it starts, is a great idea, but average executives base this play on patents alone, which don't work. Instead, look at locking up key suppliers, distributors, and talent and preempting markets by making the large expenditures necessary to come after you too great for the market opportunity.

CHAPTER TEN

DECISIONS, DECISIONS

OK, good stuff. But now, what move do I make? After the plans are identified, after the ideas crystallize, you actually have to do something.

Even very good players struggle with exactly which move to select from a list of decent choices. Without some discipline, it's easy to partially analyze lots of alternatives, get some fuzzy and muddled ideas, and suddenly realize that the clock is ticking, so you have to do something. The move currently on your mind looks sort of OK, so you make it but without the confidence that it really was the best choice.

An unfortunate number of business moves get made in just this way. But top chess players take a different approach. That process goes like this: First, "What has changed?" Second, "Do we have an active plan for change that we're pursuing, or are we just playing positionally?" Third, what are the "candidate moves"? Fourth, apply the filters described in this chapter. Finally, "check your answer": Make sure you're counting on your opponent to make his best move, that you aren't falling into a trap, and that your thought process is free of common biases. You're ready to move.

FIRST, WHAT HAS CHANGED?

In the information revolution, the rate of change is our biggest threat. The first thing to check is the feedback loop. Every decision-making process must commence with the question, "What has changed since the last time we looked at this issue?" It is nearly certain that something is different now than yesterday.

Continuing on the old path without searching hard for changes in the situation is like playing chess without bothering to look at your opponent's last move. Has a new competitor arrived? A new technology appeared? On a more pedestrian level, have we lost a big order from the sales pipeline? If so, let's get busy to find out what that might be telling us about our competitive position.

Not all changes are adverse, of course; many present new opportunities. Is that technology advancement potentially useful to us (even if it was "not invented here")? Has my opponent's last move created any weaknesses in his position, like creating a new weak square to attack?

Once we're sure we understand the current situation, it is time to move on.

SECOND, WHAT'S THAT PLAN AGAIN?

Back in Chapter 3, we discussed the process for making plans. In subsequent chapters, we addressed typical strategies chess players and good executives can consider, such as attacking the base of a pawn chain, countering a wing attack with one in the center, or playing an exchange sacrifice to deal with a wasting advantage. Meantime, early-stage ventures may be executing the Big Idea of their opening.

But here's the secret we'll admit just between ourselves: We may not really have a plan! Despite all thinking and work, we just might not see a good path forward right now. But because we know the clock is still ticking, we have to do something. But what? Chess players know the answer. They're very good at knowing what to do when you don't know what to do: Make a positional move, the kind discussed in the "First Mover" and "Bad Bishops" chapters. If you're an early-stage company, make sure you're developing your whole team rapidly and evenly, get your pieces on good ssquares, and castle early to barriers to entry. Ventures of all stages can look to improve the scope of their major pieces, eliminate bad Bishops, and ensure their pawns are moving with the right support. Make sure you're iterating the products rapidly. If nothing else is apparent, you can always find candidate moves that will reinforce your strong square: Talk to customers, interview your relationship managers, or examine your sales pipeline for trends.

THIRD, WHAT ARE OUR CANDIDATE MOVES?

Whether they're actively pursuing a directed plan or just making some positional moves, strong players always identify a short list of candidate moves, credible options for how to proceed. (As world champion Emanuel Lasker used to say, "If you see a good move, wait; there may be a better one.")

But once the short list is drawn up, how do we decide between the options quickly enough to stay ahead on the clock? One reason good players can compete with computers is that they know what moves *not* to spend time thinking about. A player will worry about the current Kingside assault rather than a subtle pawn maneuver over on the Queenside. Computers have a harder time deciding what's "important"; every possible legal move seems worth investigation, so they run down their clock while poring over moves that GMs would ignore.

Many executives suffer from this same inability to distinguish the big from the small. They feel their day is well spent so long as they're working hard, like a chess computer, on some problem or another. This trait is dangerous not only because it risks spending time on the wrong things but also because it risks spending too much time, period. Executives who consume a lot of time ensuring their fingers are in every pie are not available to members of the organization; their days are too full of trivia for them to have meaningful input. The weirdest thing is how self-satisfied these executives tend to be: If they're frazzled, they must be doing a great job. This is a horrible problem. They're actually cutting themselves off from valuable input, missing many of the changes that they really should be reacting to while instead they pore over every possible option the company has.

Thus, a disciplined approach to generating a short list of candidate moves, and then choosing between them, is essential. These moves are ones we can quickly decide are viable in ways that will move our plan along or improve our overall position if we don't have an active plan in process. No serious analysis is involved at this stage; it's a quick decision made after looking at a short list of credible options.

Fortunately, the chess gods have issued a sort of harmonic mandate for good moves, and the business gods took note: *You can nearly always be sure that a decent-looking move that fits the overall plan is, in fact, an excellent move.* That is to say, relax. Individual moves don't have to be brilliant; they just have to be consistent ("Lucky or Good?") and rhythmic ("On the Clock").

Even so, you always want to generate a list of at least three to five candidates. The best way to do this is to remember the principle of the "executive Bishop pair." If you bring together people of genuinely different perspectives, you're far more likely to generate a list of meaningfully different ideas, not just minor variations on the same theme. Once your team generates a list of several candidate moves, filter them.

FOURTH, FILTER

Here's the list of filters that allow you to choose between the moves you're looking at:

1. Favor moves that maintain the greatest possible future flexibility. Probe first, and react to the reaction. In chess, players who face an uncomfortable pin often make a simple pawn move that we say "puts the question" to the piece applying the pin. In response, it has to either exchange itself for the pinned piece (relieving the pressure) or back up to maintain the pin (when we can reevaluate how to address the problem). We don't need to go crazy trying to break the pin immediately; we test the waters first.

   Sometimes small moves like this are dismissed as not decisive or bold enough. But these kinds of testing moves are more likely to lead to ultimate success, for reasons discussed in "First Mover": They create an immediate feedback loop and the chance to rapidly iterate.

2. As discussed in "Classic Tactics," favor moves that achieve both offensive and defensive aims; this saves "tempos." Even when primarily focused on defense, try to make the opponent play your game. A strictly defensive move, like a price cut, is normally not a great one; instead, look to counter by bundling additional features or service. This not only defends the price, it turns the tables and makes the competitor react.

3. Categorize candidate moves by the amount of available information you have about them and hence how likely they are to be right. Remember, there is only that one "priority zero." All things being equal, make the move you're most certain about first. As that one plays out, clarifying information may well show up to inform your other decisions.

4. Calculate as far as possible. We have touched on this subject before, but it is so critical that we can risk a bit of redundancy. There is reality and myth in both financial analysis and chess calculation. The reality is that certain aspects of the enterprise are subject to rigorous financial analysis and even require it. The closely related myth is that spreadsheets can predict the future. We've already proved that number crunching doesn't win chess games; otherwise Deep Blue, the chess-playing computer, would always beat even the best humans. Pure number crunching also fails in business. Any financial projections (as opposed to measurements of previous events) require assumptions about a broad range of human behaviors and responses, which will in turn generate another broad set of reactions. Remember Euro Disney.

　　Financial projections are usually pretty good ways to estimate the costs of a project, and that may be enough to decide which approach is best when the upside is a complete unknown. However, they are much less reliable for predicting revenue, and they have little value in any strategic evaluation.

5. Make the move that maximizes future options. If you're still

unclear about the best move, make the one that will provide you the greatest flexibility and largest number of options in the future. *Option value* is well understood in the financial markets and by good chess players but generally underappreciated in the business strategy world. As a friend of mine says when looking at big decisions, "The goal of round one is to get to round two." So stay as light on your feet as possible.

NOW, CHECK YOUR ANSWER!

After taking the above considerations into account, you will most likely have a top candidate among your possible moves. But, just as you tell your kids that after they take a test they should go back and check the answers before the bell, there are a few things to make sure of before actually touching the piece. Did you make your decision with the following points in mind?

ALWAYS, ALWAYS EXPECT YOUR OPPONENT TO MAKE HIS BEST MOVE

One of the silliest things chess beginners do is make moves that are fundamentally unsound in the hope that their opponents won't see something. Hey, this is the information age: Everybody sees everything. You absolutely must make decisions based on the market, your competitors, and your customers seeing the consequence of your move and being very smart and self-interested in the way they react. Mr. Market, Mr. Customer, Mr. Competitor, and even Mr. Inertia are very clever fellows.

A common example is airline fare wars. A carrier cuts ticket prices to gain market share. But, of course, the move is instantly seen and matched by the opponent, negating the advantage. Usually the only result is lost revenues and profits. This kind of move doesn't address the position's fundamental issues at all (a too-high fixed cost of operation) and is extremely unlikely to result in meaningful long-term advantage.

Salesforce.com recently made a more serious version of this mistake. It had been operating a nice, growing business with a Web-based sales management tool. Aimed at small companies that didn't need to integrate their customer relationship management (CRM) systems with other back-end infrastructure, the company did not draw competition from the big players, like Oracle. But then, with great fanfare, Salesforce.com announced a string of high-profile deals with Cisco and Dell in a major thrust into the enterprise space.

To do this, Salesforce.com had to cut its per-seat pricing dramatically so that the growth produced much lower profits. But that, in itself, could have been a reasonable trade-off. The real problem was that Salesforce.com didn't consider what its opponent would do in response. After all, this amounted to an attack on Oracle's castled Kingside (Oracle had earlier purchased Seibel Systems, the grandfather of CRM applications). Sure enough, the counterattack came: a greatly souped-up version of Oracle's own on-demand sales management software, now positioned to attack Salesforce.com's own customer base. If Salesforce.com had no opponent to worry about, its growth-versus-profitability trade-off might have made sense. But thinking that Grandmaster Larry Ellison, CEO of Oracle, would allow it to go unchallenged was a blunder of the first order.

Similarly, back in the early days of satellite TV, British Satellite Broadcasting (BSB) went head to head with Rupert Murdoch's Sky Television and outbid it (at a hefty sum) for the rights to broadcast television signals back to the U.K. on a new British communications satellite. What BSB had not, apparently, thought about was how Murdoch, not exactly a timid competitor, would respond, which was to find a different satellite capable of the same thing. He simply went out and acquired rights to a Spanish bird that could also reach the U.K. BSB overlooked his countermove and, partially as a result, did not aggressively push deployment as quickly as it might have. It was flabbergasted when Sky launched more than a year earlier than BSB did.

Thinking you see a massive breakthrough can make cold-blooded analysis of the opponent's best responses difficult. Even the greatest military minds fall prey to this problem. One famous example involved the Japanese war planning for the strike on Midway Island. As they went through the war-game exercise, the Japanese reviewed a potential scenario that eventually occurred: a devastating surprise strike by U.S. dive-bombers while the Japanese warplanes were on deck refueling. If this potential had been taken more seriously and different plans been adopted, the history of the war in the Pacific might have been very different. But in the excitement about the expected wipeout of the remaining American Navy, the downside scenarios were ignored.

Still, don't get paranoid. As discussed in "Lucky or Good?" expecting your opponent to make his best move does *not* mean he'll use that move to maximally interfere with your plans. That is, there is often good news in expecting the best move from your opponent. Often he won't interfere with your plans, even though he could stop them if he so chose, because from his point of view, he's got better things to do with that move.

WATCH OUT FOR TRAPS!

Lots of people who don't play the game fantasize that chess players are always setting traps for each other. The dull truth is that they rarely do. Grandmasters are usually just too good to fall for them, and if they require that the person setting the trap take risks with his own position, the risk-reward payoff just isn't there. It is much better to just make a solid move and get on with the game.

But every once in a while a trap gets set, so we do have to pay attention. When a player sees an apparently juicy move, there are two things in particular to worry about: (1) Why is this opportunity here? Has my opponent *really* overlooked something? (2) Will seizing this short-term opportunity hurt my long-term position?

Why Is This Opportunity Here?

You should have a chess player's skepticism when examining an apparently big new business opportunity. Not to say that our capital markets system is perfect, but it's pretty darn good. It's uncommon for it to overlook something. Therefore, before jumping into a new business or investing in one, it's always best to ask: "Why is this opportunity here?"

Recently, I met with folks from a great little company that had started a niche athletic clothing business. They'd gotten some early traction in a particular sport, and their order flow was improving quickly. What made it a really fascinating opportunity was that the company had obtained the rights from a university for a new antimicrobial agent that promised to kill a huge variety of fungi and bacteria. Imagine, athletic apparel that keeps you from getting athlete's foot and kills odor at the same time.

Could it be? I had the patent applications reviewed by an experienced chemist and ex-patent officer. Sure enough, the basic approach was sound. Moreover, the process didn't work on a metabolic basis, so there was no risk of encouraging mutations into supergerms. Instead, it acted as detergent that simply broke down the cell walls in a brute force approach. The substance would permanently bond to the surface of most fabrics, being undisturbed by soap and water. Nor did dryer-type heat levels have any effect.

Now, most of us are suckers for optimism (certainly I am), and that's a good, constructive thing. But in chess and business, allowing yourself to get carried away by enthusiasm usually leads to problems. If you think you see a several-move mating combination that involves sacrificing a few pieces along the way, you have to study each step deeply to see what unexpected defensive move can save the other side (it is this trait, in particular, that makes playing computers so annoying: Somehow, they always dig up a wacky defensive tactic that stymies your gorgeous idea).

If you've suddenly come across a miracle business opportunity, even with new technology at its root, the same caution applies. The single best test for this in the business world is, Does the company have competition? If the answer is no, be very, very careful. Rarely will you find a genuine opportunity so novel that no one else is doing it.

No one is marketing anti-athlete's foot socks. Why not? It made us rethink the whole situation. Eventually the core problem did emerge. Yes, the new product would stand up to soap and water, but that was only part of the story. Today's detergents are loaded with all sorts of enzymes and oxidation agents, and those enzymes like to dine on the exact types of molecules that were the basis of the whole approach behind the antimicrobial apparel. So, just one washing in the family load would neutralize the antimicrobial agent. "Well, shoot fire!" (as we used to say in the South). That was the end of that.

In the same vein, to tell one of many possible tales on myself, early on I was so blinded by enthusiasm for a 3D camera that I simply forgot the core question: What, exactly, was anybody going to do with it? We searched high and low and came close a couple of times with ideas as far-ranging as creating virtual body doubles for Hollywood and scanning architectural features of old buildings. We actually did license it to Minolta for use in a short-lived consumer camera. But none of these really supported a business. I should have been much more diligent in asking why the 3D camera opportunity existed and *why there was no competition*. My assumption had been that the science was a big breakthrough, but that was only partly correct. A better answer was that there had not been enough of a potential market for the product for anyone to care.

A more well-known example of this problem is the Segway personal transportation device. It is a cool invention, and it works. The bad news is that it has no competition. Like our revolutionary 3D camera, too many people have to change too many things in their lives to generate widespread adoption. For Segway, there are numerous physical barriers to using the device, not to mention the basic etiquette questions of running over people's toes on New York City sidewalks. We already have good-enough ways of moving around (like walking), so that the radical changes required to use a Segway just don't seem worth it. There's no natural place for the invention to plug in and get used quickly and broadly.

A little competition, on the other hand, almost always means some sort of developed market where at least the most basic adoption problems have been overcome. So whenever an entrepreneur beams, "We really have no competition," watch out! It could be a trap.

Is This a Short-Term Gain?

Chess offers countless examples of the folly of taking short-term gains that cause long-term pains. For example, as discussed in "First

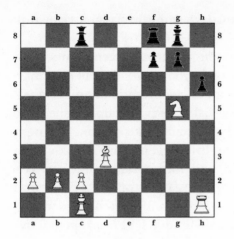

END-OF-QUARTER TEMPTATION

Mover," charging the Queen around the board early to pick off a couple of stray pawns nearly always sets the stage for defeat: Those moves need to be used to develop your team instead. Take a look at this diagram.

Black is already winning and can grind out a victory. But White's Knight can be taken right now without fear of recapture. And you can be sure that lots of CEOs, near the end of a quarter and looking for a pop, would take it. Yes, we can grab it and report a great quarter: captured Knights up 100 percent!

Juicy as it is, this revenue addition causes major disruption to the organization, removing that pawn from its normal job of plugging up the h file. And, sure enough, that will cost Black the game.[1]

Nearly always, taking the short-term gain at the end of a quarter by selling off an asset, offering a deal outside the normal business model, or accelerating sales by radically cutting prices will similarly lead to adverse consequences. The damage is sometimes subtle but nonetheless real: A move like that indicates a lack of confidence in the plan, which resonates all too loudly throughout the lower tiers of the organization (oh, yes, everybody gets it). Or that special deal will often carry with it ongoing management and support issues that don't reflect in the income statement but take a real toll on the company's future effectiveness. In short: Leave the Knight alone.

ADMIT BUT DON'T DWELL ON YOUR MISTAKES

Probably because they don't live in a political system, good chess players are much better than executives at one thing above all:

acknowledging that they've missed something and adjusting accordingly.

Once you've spent time devising a plan and several moves on implementing it, the hardest thing in the world is to acknowledge that you've overlooked something, that something is amiss. You'll frequently see intermediate players, shocked by an opponent's sudden and unforeseen seizure of a valuable piece, make the next move of their previously existing plan even more quickly than usual, as if nothing untoward had happened. Somehow the thought is that if you just keep moving quickly, you'll prove you were right all along. It is common in the business world as well.

The most obvious example is the tendency of bankers to waive covenants and even extend new capital to troubled borrowers. Having literally invested so much in a decision, it becomes much easier to invest a little more in the hope of a turnaround than it is to acknowledge the earlier mistake. Usually, as in chess, this just leads to faster deterioration of the position.

The lesson here is to do what good players do: Admit your mistake to yourself and come up with a new plan immediately. Dropping a Rook for a Bishop is a problem and might even eventually lose the game. But it also might not, if new, realistic plans are generated quickly enough. Bishops have their own strengths and can even be superior to Rooks in certain kinds of situations, so we now have to steer for one of those. Plunging ahead as if nothing has happened, whether out of pride, bluff, or fear, is disastrous.

Remember ESPN's attempt to enter the cell phone market? Having had tremendous success in expanding its brand from television to magazines by essentially launching a new product especially for its own existing customers, rather than by trying to pry readers from other existing magazines, it tried to replicate the trick in the cell phone industry. That seemed logical enough, but it didn't work. The barriers to entry were too high because getting users to switch cell phone services was a heck of a lot harder than having them buy another magazine.

But the good news was, ESPN figured it out pretty quickly and made the best of a bad situation: It gained significant knowledge about what people did and didn't want on their mobile devices and has incorporated that knowledge into its latest, and very promising, "third screen" initiative, delivering video and other content to cell phones. So it got a little something out of it after all, although probably not worth the cost. But the damage was limited.

Another example is Creative Technology, one of the companies that had pioneered sound cards for PCs. It leveraged this expertise into becoming the original leader in MP3 players: In 1999, it launched the Nomad portable player a full two years ahead of Apple's iPod and dominated the market. But when Apple did enter the fray, it arrived with a spectacularly better user experience, given the iTunes software and music library, and of course, a much cooler product. On seeing this move, the Creative Technology CEO, Sim Wong Hoo, refused to admit the quality of his opponent's move and doubled down. He declared that the iPod was "worse than the cheapest Chinese player" and launched a multi-million-dollar advertising campaign to defend a product that clearly, to everyone outside the company, indefensible. After several years of resulting losses, the scorecard stood: Apple, 25 percent of the worldwide market; Creative Technology, 6 percent.

But there could be a happy ending. Creative Technology then recognized the obvious and is now trying to deal with the new reality rather than deny it. The company launched the first of what is expected to be a long line of iPod accessory products, the xDock, which moves music wirelessly from an iPod to any speakers in the house. The great thing about this move is that it capitalizes on a strength the company has always had—superior digital sound—in a way that accurately takes account of the current situation. While some analysts squawk, claiming the product may undermine the image of the company's own music players, those guys are making the same mistake Hoo originally made and the same one beginning chess players make all the time: failing to respect that opponents, too, come up with great ideas and execute them.

In these situations, it's best to remember how the economist John Maynard Keynes, reputed to be a fair chess player, responded when asked what he did when presented with evidence that one of his pet theories was wrong. He reportedly replied, "I change my mind. What do you do, sir?"

The flip side is to dwell on mistakes, to get caught in the emotional trap of obsessing about how much better off we'd be today "if only." Often this results in trying too hard to get back to where we think we could have been. That mind-set, in turn, almost always leads to overly optimistic (or underly negative, if you prefer) analysis of the current position and likely outcomes. Recent studies have shown how humans' aversion to loss results in yet-bigger losses through this mechanism, called "gambler's syndrome." Remember, like a good player, that the board position now is the board position now; all you can ever do is play it from here in the best possible way.

Bad decisions are inevitable. The only people who've never failed are those who haven't tried to do anything beyond their comfort zone, hardly a prescription for progress. That you'll make mistakes is a given. The past is the past; let it go.

LESSONS

A business GM makes decisions about particular moves by:

1. Beginning every evaluation session by asking "what's different now?" and incorporating those data into any existing plans.
2. Generating candidate moves, either to further an affirmative plan of change or to simply improve the position.
3. Filtering these based primarily on flexibility, "option value," and to a limited extent, financial projections.
4. Checking the answer: making sure you're anticipating the opponent's best possible response and checking for traps.

And finally,

5. Don't let blown opportunities and previous mistakes unduly influence you. Everybody who's trying makes mistakes. All that matters is the current reality; just play the board as it sits.

A Postgame Recap

A startling difference between the world of chess and the world of business concerns the willingness to learn from mistakes. Good chess players live and die playing over their old games, but executives rarely conduct a serious review of why certain things went wrong unless the real point is to assign blame.

And they essentially never look back when things go well. The implication is that every decision that yields a positive result was a good one, but that's just wrong. Chess players and businesspeople "win" games riddled with errors for all sorts of reasons. Never mistake a good outcome for your own brilliance: There is always much to learn from analyses of both failed and successful projects.

After the first game of the 1992 World Chess Championship, which Garry Kasparov won handily, he surprised me by asking me over to his apartment for a bite. The surprise was simply that after an exhausting effort, I'd thought he would want to get in as much sleep as possible before the next game. So I figured I'd stop over, visit with his wonderful mother, Clara, enjoy something from the Russian buffet she always had at the ready, then quickly clear out.

Instead, when the door opened, a score of Russian Grandmasters started shouting variations and questions at Garry. It sounded like the floor of the CBOE. No boards were needed; everybody knew the game just played so incredibly well that they could simply start rattling off hypothetical moves as quickly and easily as they could name their own relatives. Others would object a few moves deep: sure, the first few moves suggested were right, but if d5 (on, say, the sixth or seventh move), then obviously Ng5, followed by g6 and Be7. Usually Garry would calmly say that, yes, he'd considered that variation, but instead of g6, he feared e4 and Rb2, with an unclear situation to follow. (By far the most comical aspect of this scene was Garry's insistence that everyone speak English so that I could follow the thread, which was like suggesting that because we share a native tongue, I can understand Steven Hawking.)

This went on deep into the night. The game was replayed a hundred times, not just the actual moves but every possible variation of the real game, many moves deep. The intensity was unbelievable: here was the greatest player in history scouring the game for hours with a cadre of other superstar players, asking, "Where could I have improved? What did I miss? What can I learn?"

After all, he had won the game! (You should have seen the process on that extremely rare occasion when he actually lost.) Conversely, I simply cannot imagine an American businessman or businesswoman putting this kind of work into reviewing a successful project—lots of pats on the back, yes, and certainly a fancy closing dinner, but not a serious effort to understand what had gone right and why.

Well, I never did get my cabbage, but I did get the point.

And in that vein, it's probably a good idea to recap the basic points we've tried to make here and the most important ideas that you can take away into your business life.

BIG IDEA, SMALL MOVES

You need a clear Big Idea aimed at creating a difference in the position, an advantage to exploit. But exactly how it will get executed, what moves will be made in what order, is beyond our power to predict, so don't waste time trying. You don't need a four-inch-thick document full of detailed financial projections to operate the business, but you do need to make sure that everyone in your organization knows the "idea behind the business plan."

To execute the idea, you'll need to move rapidly but rhythmically: no passing, but no panic. *You're on the clock.* So create a product infrastructure and a culture that enables and expects regular change. You'll also need maximum effectiveness from your team, ensuring that each piece is put on the right square that will allow it maximum scope, pawns included. Exchange ineffective pieces immediately.

As the Big Idea is implemented, it is certain that new plans will be required. *But they should always key off the positive imbalance that the Big Idea created.* Given that imbalance, imagine a dream strategic position in the industry and, in doing so, don't rely on financial calculations or forward projections of the markets. Doing that is acting like a chess computer. You're a human.

One of the best business chess plans is to create a strong square. These are narrow market niches over which a company can exert control, not to be confused with mere core competencies. Properly overprotected, strong squares will be a constant source of new revenues, customers, and product innovation. And don't mistake this strength for the delivery mechanism or platform you use. Those change (especially these days), but the customer relationships that underlie strong squares should be transportable.

No Advantage Lasts Forever

No advantage lasts forever, so the trick is to exchange it for one of a different sort while it still has enough value that you'll get a meaningful new advantage in return. In particular, business models get tired, so be prepared to junk the old one to create a new method of extracting value from your strong squares. Sac the exchange.

Chess offers many concrete examples of how to attack markets and competitors. Whatever else, *make sure to strike at a weak spot;* no matter how good you are, don't bother attacking a fully fortified area. Find a chink in the armor, maybe the base of a pawn chain. If one isn't apparent, try to create one by pushing a disruptive model in a minority attack. "Open up" and recruit the power of the outside world to your side.

The best defense is a good offense. Find a way to get the initiative—in particular, to meet an attack on the wing, strike back in the middle of the market. Block your opponents with prophylaxis, but remember that patents alone won't work. *Do not play "pure" defense;* cost cutting alone is not a strategy.

Remember that making decisions in the information age requires some short-handing; as in chess, *it is impossible to fully analyze every possibility, so don't try.* Generate a few candidate moves that are consistent with your Big Idea, apply the filters, and move without trying to be perfect; you'll be moving again soon enough. But always expect your opponent to make his best possible move in response, and do watch out for traps.

FINALLY, ALWAYS REPLAY EVENTS WITH A CRITICAL EYE

Don't just look back to find your mistakes in your losses: your wins have as much to teach you. Life, like chess, is all about learning so we'll do better next time.

NOTES

Preface

1. Richard Eales, *Chess, The History of a Game* (B.T. Batsford Ltd, Great Britain, 1985), p. 66.

Chapter Two

1. Thomas L. Friedman, *The World Is Flat* (Farrar, Straus, and Giroux, U.S.A., 2005).
2. Malcolm Gladwell, *The Tipping Point* (Little, Brown & Co., 2000).
3. Clayton M. Christensen, *The Innovator's Dilemma* (Harvard Business School Press, 1997).
4. Nassim Nicholas Taleb, *The Black Swan* (Random House, 2007).
5. Phil Rosenzweig, *The Halo Effect* (Free Press, 2007).

Chapter Three

1. Nick De Firmian, *Modern Chess Openings, 14th Edition* (Random House, Puzzles & Games, 1999).
2. *Forbes*, Sept. 18, 2006.
3. Clayton M. Christensen and Michael E. Raynor, *The Innovator's Solution* (Harvard Business School Publishing Corporation, 2003), p. 231.

Chapter Six

1. Brian Quinn, *Strategies for Change* (Richard D. Irwin, Inc., Homewood, Ill., 1980), p. 52.
2. Peter Drucker, *The Essential Drucker* (CollinsBusiness, 2001), p. 31.
3. *New York Times*, June 17, 2007.
4. Rita Gunther McGrath and Ian C. MacMillan, "Discovery-Driven Planning," *Harvard Business Review*, July 1, 1995.
5. To try to adjust for this problem, modern chess computers have a much more sophisticated evaluation system than just a point-count method to help them decide whether a position they "see" down

the road is a good one. Strategic factors like open files, doubled pawns, and the like are assigned values. But there's no such thing for business, so don't count on any numbers-based approach to generate a great long-term game plan for your company.

6. Jeremy Silman, *How to Reassess Your Chess, 3rd Edition* (Siles Press, Los Angeles, 1993).

7. Id., p. 27.

8. Aron Nimzowitsch, *My System, 21st Century Edition* (Hays Publishing, 1991), p. 23.

Chapter Seven

1. *Business Week,* Nov. 13, 2006, p. 47.

2. Aron Nimzowitsch, *My System, 21st Century Edition* (Hays Publishing, 1991), p. 154.

3. *New York Times,* June 17, 2007, Business section, p. 3.

Chapter Eight

1. Chris Zook, *Profit From the Core* (Harvard Business School Press, 2001).

2. Andrew S. Grove, *Only the Paranoid Survive* (Profile Business, 1998).

Chapter Nine

1. Ludûk Pachman, *Modern Chess Strategy* (Dover Publications, 1963), p. 285.

2. *New York Times,* Nov. 12, 2007, p. C2.

3. Ludûk Pachman, *Modern Chess Strategy* (Dover Publications, 1963), p. 291.

Chapter Ten

1. The problem is that taking the Knight with the h6 pawn opens the h file for the White Rook. Therefore, White can go Bishop to h7 with check on his next turn, forcing the Black King to h8. Then, White retreats his Bishop to f5 . . . this simultaneously attacks the Black Queen and "discovers" a check with the Rook on the now-open h file. Black has to move his King back to g8 and thus loses his Queen. Short-term gain, long-term pain.

About the Author

Bob Rice (Short Hills, NJ) began his career as a trial attorney at the U.S. Justice Department, and then served as a partner at Wall Street's prestigious Milbank, Tweed, Hadley, and McCloy for many years. He left to start a software venture that was purchased by a NASDAQ company of which he later became CEO. He is currently a Managing Partner of Tangent Capital, which structures financial products for hedge funds, and a member of the New York Angels venture finance group. Along the way, Bob served as Commissioner of the Professional Chess Association, founded the Wall Street Chess Club, ran numerous international chess events, and produced a successful "speedchess" series for ESPN.

INDEX